RUDOLF STEINER (1861–1925) called his spiritual philosophy 'anthroposophy', meaning 'wisdom of the human being'. As a highly developed seer, he based his work on direct knowledge and perception of spiritual dimensions. He initiated a modern and universal 'science of spirit', accessible to anyone willing to exercise clear and unprejudiced thinking. From his spiritual investigations Steiner provided suggestions for the renewal of many activities, including education (both general and special), agriculture, medicine, economics, architecture, science, philosophy, religion and the arts. Today there are thousands of schools, clinics, farms and other organizations involved in practical work based on his principles. His many published works feature his research into the spiritual nature of the human being, the evolution of the world and humanity, and methods of personal development. Steiner wrote some 30 books and delivered over 6000 lectures across Europe. In 1924 he founded the General Anthroposophical Society, which today has branches throughout the world.

The Tempest.
The Winters Tale.
The Life of Henry the Fift.
Much adoe about Nothing.
The Tragedie of Julius Cæsar.
Twelfe Night, or, What you will.
The Tragedie of Romeo and Juliet.
The second Part of Henry the Sixt.
The two Gentlemen of Verona.
The Life and Death of Richard the Third.
The life and death of King John.
Anthony and Cleopatra. The Life of King Henry the Eight. The first Part of Henry the Sixt.
Pericles Prince of Tyre.
The Tragedie of Titus Andronicus.
Loues Labour's lost.
The Tragedie of Hamlet.
Timon of Athens.
As you like it.
The Taming of the Shrew.
Measure for Measure.
The life and death of Richard the second. The Tragedie of Macbeth.
All's Well, that Ends Well.
The Comedie of Errors.
The First Part of King Henry the Fourth.
The Tragedie of Cymbeline.
The Tragedie of Coriolanus.
The Tragedie of King Lear.
The Tragedie of Othello.
The third Part of King Henry the Sixt.
The second Part of King Henry the Fourth.
The Merchant of Venice.
A Midsommer nights Dreame.
The Merry Wiues of Windsor.
The Tragedie of Troylus and Cressida.

A. GAMES

Abram Games © Estate of Abram Games 1975,
reproduced by kind permission

SHAKESPEARE

BECOMING HUMAN

RUDOLF STEINER

Edited with an introduction by Andrew Wolpert

RUDOLF STEINER PRESS

Rudolf Steiner Press,
Hillside House, The Square
Forest Row, RH18 5ES

www.rudolfsteinerpress.com

Published by Rudolf Steiner Press 2016

© Rudolf Steiner Press 2016
Introduction © Andrew Wolpert 2016

Earlier versions of the lectures by Rudolf Steiner have been published in the following volumes: lecture 1 in *What is Necessary in These Urgent Times*, SteinerBooks 2010, translated by Rory Bradley; lecture 2 in *Old and New Methods of Initiation*, Rudolf Steiner Press 1991, translated by Johanna Collis; lecture 3 in *Waldorf Education and Anthroposophy*, Vol. 1, Anthroposophic Press 1995, translator unknown

All rights reserved. Apart from any fair dealing for the purpose of private study, research, criticism or review, as permitted under the Copyright, Designs and Patents Act, 1988, no part of this publication may be reproduced, stored in a retrieval system, or transmitted in any form or by any means, electronic, electrical, chemical, mechanical, optical, photocopying, recording or otherwise, without the prior written permission of the copyright owner. Inquiries should be addressed to the Publishers

A catalogue record for this book is available from the British Library

Print book ISBN: 978 1 85584 524 4
Ebook ISBN: 978 1 85584 476 6

Cover by Morgan Creative featuring photo of sculpture © Tony Bagget
Typeset by DP Photosetting, Neath, West Glamorgan
Printed and bound by 4Edge Ltd., Essex

Contents

Introduction	1
Affinities	1
Becoming human	4
Some references by Rudolf Steiner to Shakespeare	14
Commentary on lectures Rudolf Steiner gave in 1922	18
Lecture 1 Dornach, 1 February 1920	27
Lecture 2 Dornach, 24 February 1922	47
Lecture 3 Stratford-on-Avon, 23 April 1922	67
Rudolf Steiner's Report on the Stratford Shakespeare Festival in 1922	85
Editor's Acknowledgements	87

Introduction

Affinities

The love for Shakespeare and recognition I have for what he represents in our culture and in a world context arises directly out of my understanding of the whole impulse in Rudolf Steiner's work. The significance of the circumstances we are born into, the challenges of the inherited social structures, the emancipation and sovereignty of the individual, the courage for the truth, the meaning of evil, the spiritual context of our biography, the reality of forgiveness and reconciliation, the creation of a new social order, and the power of unconditional love, all these occur again and again in Shakespeare's work; their beauty and truth are universally acknowledged and enjoyed. The spiritual science that arises out of Rudolf Steiner's work allows all these soul-nourishing experiences also to become amenable to a level of conscious understanding, so that our engagement with the plays, not just as actors and directors, but also as students and members of an audience can become a co-creative participation in the redemptive potential of Shakespeare's work.

Rudolf Steiner describes the stages in our human evolution, the necessary separation from our spiritual origins, and the possibility of finding a new connection to the cosmos. He affirms again and again the pivotal cosmic-human-earthly event when a Divine Being incarnated into human life on earth. Christ experienced human earthly death, overcame the consequences of that, and brought to humanity the possibility of becoming free and creating a new connection to the spiritual world. Rudolf Steiner refers to these original Easter events as the Mystery of Golgotha. The reality of this turning point, everywhere explicit in anthroposophy, is everywhere implicit in Shakespeare's work. Its universally recognizable (and globally recognized) human appeal affirms the spiritual, essential humanness of Shakespeare's work that needs no explicit religious framework. This has an affinity with anthroposophy; here Christianity transcends the denominationalism of a Church and becomes a spiritual reality synonymous with nothing less than the truly human. This celebration of the human and our potential to achieve it is the very heart of Shakespeare's work. Anthroposophy is exactly this celebration of our becoming human, and at its heart is Christ, the Archetypal Human Being, who shows us through his Deed what we can become.

Rudolf Steiner spoke about the mighty events in the spiritual world that accompanied the beginnings of our modern age, the arts of the Renaissance in Europe, the development of science and technology, the beginnings of industrialization in Britain and the rise of materialism. He spoke about a gathering in the spiritual world of all those human and angelic beings who felt responsible for a coming period of culture on earth when it would be realized that the methods of natural science could be applied also to supersensible experiences. When the objective enquiry into external natural phenomena had taught us how to be scientists, we could apply that method of enquiry in the no less objective relationship we can develop to our inner experiences of soul and spirit. That is the basis of the epistemology of spiritual science, anthroposophy.

It becomes increasingly clear that so much of the art of the Renaissance, for example of Michelangelo, Raphael and Leonardo in Italy and of Shakespeare a hundred years later in Britain, comes from this momentous spiritual gathering, a great symposium, a school in heaven. Rudolf Steiner characterizes this as the cosmic source of an impulse that leads human beings on earth to a free and conscious knowing of our spiritual dimension, not a belief, but an understanding of reincarnation, destiny and a vision of our human potential.[1] This supersensible school was under the leadership of the Archangel Michael, one of whose chief concerns is that we should be free, and that we should know who we are and what we can achieve. All this art of the sixteenth and seventeenth centuries is like an open secret, revealing in architecture, sculpture, painting, poetry and drama, for those who want to know, so much of what then comes in the twentieth century through the spiritual research of Rudolf Steiner. It is as if some of what Rudolf Steiner brings in the twentieth century in ideas, thoughts and words, primarily (but by no means exclusively) in language, had already been brought into public culture through the visual and stage arts more than 400 years before. Artists are prophets, and exactly where they appealed to our sense of beauty Rudolf Steiner appeals to our cognitive faculties, our sense of truth.

So often it is in relationship to Goethe that Rudolf Steiner speaks about Shakespeare, in connection with the evolution of the arts of poetry and drama, the transitions between cultural epochs, and the cosmic origins and the connections with the past. Then in the last lecture (see page 83) Rudolf Steiner explicitly acknowledges the universal relevance of Shakespeare for the whole world and for the future.

Out of these considerations I venture to say that my appreciation of the grandeur and depth of Shakespeare arises more out of my recognition of anthroposophy as a whole than out of the specific things Rudolf Steiner says about Shakespeare. There is an immense affinity between what breathes through Shakespeare and what shines through Rudolf Steiner. In this introduction I begin by expanding on some of the relevant themes in Shakespeare's work with reference to some of the central themes in anthroposophy before giving consideration to the references Rudolf Steiner makes to Shakespeare in his lectures and the inclusion of three of them in the main part of this publication.

Becoming human

An evolving imagination of the human being reveals itself through the progress of the plays. This section exemplifies some aspects of that with a selection of references to illustrate this development.

In the history plays Shakespeare presents us with a very particular view of monarchs, kings that have for different reasons lost their sovereignty. These plays offer a view of an old hierarchical social structure that may still outwardly be powerful, but is bereft of any inner authority. And yet in *Richard II*, for example, something additional becomes visible. Richard knows his weakness and is also sensitive enough to realize the reality of Henry's position. We see the poignant struggle between the weaknesses of the personality and the deeper intuitive glimpses of the individual, and all this against the background of the polarity between the anachronism of being 'God's anointed' and the realpolitik of power and ambition. This is not the sixteenth-century consciousness reflecting on the fourteenth-century events. This struggle, not against Henry, but within Richard between the expectations from the past, the demands of the present and the helpless vacillating between them is a modern biographical issue, and so sensitively, lyrically and non-didactically presented.

In *King Lear* we see a monarch who is truly sovereign; the King of France makes a brief 'homoeopathic' appearance at the beginning and then works through Cordelia and the sovereignty she at the end brings to her father. This sovereignty does not arise out of an inherited social structure. The King of France manifests selfless, unconditional love and, as an archetype of individuality rather than personality, has no name. In the context of Rudolf Steiner's description of the human ego, we can recognize the King of France as the true self that awakens the everyday consciousness in Cordelia to her higher self, and the almost selfless nobility of Kent as an individual who has already awoken to his higher self. When Lear, maddened and bereft of his knights, his crown and all outer trappings, encounters his naked godson feigning madness in the storm, there he recognizes what the human being is, 'unaccommodated man'. He has foolishly and unwittingly initiated the wise but pitifully painful process that leads to this self-knowledge. What the King of France knows at the beginning King Lear has to discover through error, blindness, fury, rejection, and then majestically in the drama of the elements.

In the Roman plays we are offered a parody of what the individual can be. Brutus, Antony and Coriolanus all show how corrupted they are and the hollowness of their outer shows of strength. Such rather general assertions certainly deserve more exemplification than this context allows, but the infinite subtleties here do merit at least one mention. It is interesting to compare how Romeo, Rosalind (*As You Like It*), Mowbray and Henry (both in *Richard II*) all react to being banished. However, what eventually becomes the hubris of Coriolanus and, even if he has not the strength later to fully live in these words, he is able to articulate this refreshingly unexpected perspective when he says, being exiled from Rome:

> I banish you ... there is a world elsewhere. (Act III, Scene III).

Even if in Coriolanus this is a sad parody of a future world-consciousness that will later be able to embrace homelessness, here spoken by a 'man' whose terrible strength is then utterly undone by his mother, it is nevertheless a magnificent harbinger of our becoming free from the constraints of our place of birth. And it is simply so that we can already see and say things that we cannot yet do. This can be seen as either weak, or as a glimpse of what we still have to strive for. Then indeed the Histories and the Roman plays do not merely portray a sad past, but also show how the future begins to make itself known as part of the flawed, incomplete condition we are in.

Many of the early comedies are characterized by the happy endings that seem to be given by convenient coincidences or the intervention of benevolent extraneous forces. For the purposes of this section it might be sufficient to acknowledge that in these plays a kind of providence, destiny, or good fortune sees to it that all turns out well, and that the protagonists experience this resolution as something given. In the late comedies the recognition, forgiveness and reconciliation have to be struggled for, sometimes against the odds and in the face of apparently unavoidable loss. When the resolution at length occurs there is mutuality and a delightful interdependence among the characters in the ensuing harmony that has certainly been striven for and won—it is achieved, not given.

Between these early and late comedies lie the tragedies. In the following section we will consider how Rudolf Steiner characterizes the proximity of the spiritual world for some of these protagonists. Here I would like to relate an aspect of esoteric Christianity to the 'tragic' nature of these plays. An essential aspect of the phenomenon of evil in the light of anthroposophy is that it is not simply a binary opposite of good. The different ways it manifests all have a rightful task within the whole context of evolution. There are various spiritual beings that challenge and threaten our true humanity, and our evolution needs such opposition against which we can grow. These 'fallen angels' also long to be redeemed and are not beyond redemption. This is a complex theme that can be dealt with here only in broad terms, and these few remarks must not be taken as comprehensively dealing with so profound a subject. In his many commentaries on Goethe's *Faust*, Rudolf Steiner characterizes the very different roles that Mephistopheles has, and shows that this single personification of the devil in reality consists of more than one being. In Shakespeare's plays there is no single character that represents evil; such weaknesses as ambition, arrogance, brutal selfishness, illusion, fear, revenge and deceit are all parts of the various 'incomplete' human beings that struggle with their deficiencies.

In an early play, *Titus Andronicus*, Shakespeare presents us with a character that embodies unmitigated and unrepentant evil. We are shown in Aaron a gratuitous bestiality that is hardly imaginable. That this level of inhumanity, apparently beyond redemption, exists must be acknowledged at the beginning of Shakespeare's progress through our evolution. But in the plays that follow, the characters who manifest inhumanity, cruelty and selfishness also carry traces of something more.

Claudius, the opportunist who commits fratricide, is driven by Hamlet's staging of the play within the play to repent, and yet he knows being pardoned is incompatible with retaining the fruits of his crime. When he rises from what he considers to have been a futile attempt at prayer he concedes:

> My words fly up, my thoughts remain below,
> Words without thoughts never to heaven go (Act III, Scene III)

The villain Claudius has a degree of honest self-knowledge, a state of grace, *pace* all his wickedness, that brings him much closer to the divine than he realizes.

There is maybe more than one explanation for Hamlet's inability to kill his uncle immediately, but when he and Laertes have fatally wounded each other, in this co-presence of impending death, they exchange forgiveness. Then Hamlet can kill his uncle, not obeying his father's wish for revenge, but now because he has his own reasons. It no longer is a question of family honour, but now a personal matter. And may we not at least consider it possible that Hamlet's initial inability to execute a blood vendetta, weakness though he himself considers it, is actually a healthy reluctance, an at first inexplicable but actually a very noble distaste for such a deed.

The shamelessly selfish, conspiring opportunist in *King Lear* is Edmund. When he is mortally wounded but not yet dead and realizes what has befallen their tortured father, he too is moved to repent:

> Some good I mean to do, despite of mine own nature
> (Act V, Scene III)

Such an impulse would have been entirely unpredictable on the basis of his track record; his wish to atone is at odds with everything we know about him. Yet here Shakespeare invites us to consider that in even such a character, facing death, a selfless urge can arise. Such a moment affirms something inestimably human; it gives courage that the future does not necessarily have to be the predictable continuation of the past.

The evil in *Othello* needs a longer span of time to reveal its longing to be relieved. When Iago leaves the stage he is unrepentant, but when this villainous character 'reappears' in

Cymbeline as Iachimo, perpetrates his scheming mischief, and then, faced with the horror of what he has done, begs to be killed as punishment, Posthumus can say to him;

> The power that I have on you is to spare you;
> The malice towards you to forgive you. Live,
> And deal with others better (Act V, Scene V)

The contrition in Iachimo inspires the forgiveness in Posthumus. This, as has been noted, is characteristic of the resolutions in the last comedies, a mutuality, a harmonious consort of recognition and reconciliation.

And then Shakespeare takes all this to another level in *The Tempest*. Prospero has committed the Lear-like folly of abdicating his responsibilities as Duke of Milan but wants to retain the title and privileges while he pursues his questionable studies of rough magic. This awakens an opportunism in his brother Antonio, who usurps him and sends him into exile with his three-year-old daughter. For twelve years Prospero harbours vengeful intentions against his brother, and is finally able to bring him within his power. But there is a deeper core of humanity in Prospero that he himself does not at first acknowledge till Ariel, who has divined it, reflects it to him.

> Ariel: . . . your affections
>   Would become tender.
> Prospero: Dost thou think so, spirit?
> Ariel: Mine would, sir, were I human.
> Prospero: And mine shall.
>   Hast thou, which art but air, a touch, a feeling
>   Of their affections, and shall not myself,

Introduction 11

> One of their kind, that relish all as sharply
> Passion as they, be kindlier mov'd than thou art?
> Though with their high wrongs I am struck to the quick,
> Yet with my nobler reason 'gainst my fury
> Do I take part: the rarer action is
> In virtue than in vengeance. (Act V, Scene I)

Prospero's two half-lines at the beginning of this extract in both cases complete the iambic pentameters begun by Ariel. This synchronicity, mutuality, inseparable immediacy that is expressed in the integrity of the poetic form is the consequence of Ariel's having been so bound to Prospero that he has taken up the deepest longings of his master's soul and now shows them to him.

Prospero rises to another level of humanity. Ariel has served him in a way he unconsciously longed for, and now he can free Ariel. He abjures his rough magic, pardons Antonio unilaterally without knowing whether his brother repents or is ready to be forgiven, and owns his connection with Caliban. It is his unconditional forgiveness of a brother that makes Prospero Shakespeare's greatest hero. Whatever people may fondly imagine, Shakespeare initially presents us in Prospero with an irresponsible, manipulative, oppressive and vindictive sorcerer. It is despite all this that he rises to the highest human potential of unconditional love, an achievement every one of us with all our all too human flaws can recognize and be encouraged by. The role that Miranda with her growing needs over twelve times twelve months plays in the education of her father would be a study in itself. It is what Prospero manages to achieve at the end that makes him a true Master, enacting on earth with others what lives as a spiritual potential.

Prospero's deed points to a future vision of humanity that we can already glimpse and maybe sometimes even achieve. This brotherliness also lives in the reconciliation between the old fathers at the end of *Romeo and Juliet*, which nought but the tragic deaths of their children can bring about. In a strange and terrible way, their children's death is the 'gift' that comes to them from outside themselves and that enables them to take a new step. There is no outward show of religion in this episode, and yet it truly is a Resurrection moment when these old men take hands and their eyes meet over the bodies of their children, their children whose love and recognition of each other defied parental prejudices. Something supremely human rises above the grief; the human beings realize the possibility of something new. It is indeed a blinkered view that sees this play only as a tragedy.

With Prospero that new step arises from within himself. Whether his spontaneous forgiveness actually leads to reconciliation with his brother is strangely, wonderfully, left open by Shakespeare. The response to such a free deed cannot be scripted. This openness between the brothers and what at the end through the Epilogue is left open between Prospero and the audience evokes a profound response from our own creative urge. The written happy endings of the early and also of the three late comedies allow us to receive what we know is right and good; we are grateful the circle is completed for us in the art. However, the true next step of *The Tempest* is ours to offer Prospero. Here lives the dissolution, not now of the boundary in consciousness between dreams and reality, but of the distinction in the theatre between actors and audience. The world has become the stage in our co-responsibility for what happens next in our as-yet-unachieved humanity.

Like so much of Renaissance art, Shakespeare's work bears an open secret. The esoteric spiritual content is undisguised, though it may be unexpected and not always immediately recognized. And like all the great artistic achievements that are inspired in this earthly renaissance of what was living in the cosmic School of Michael, this work remains incomplete until we recognize and respond to its open invitation, its deepest longing, indeed its urgent expectation that we become active participants.

If the great impulse in Shakespeare's work is the celebration of the individual in the quest to become free, conscious and co-responsible in the creation of a world where human dignity, courage for the truth, and love are sovereign, then it would be blatantly inartistic and morally deceitful for the author to hide his true identity. If we recognize the morality and the worthy idealism in this work of art, it is only such intrinsic criteria of internal consistency that can vouchsafe the identity of the author. The times when anonymity and pseudonymity were necessary and acceptable in our culture are past. If this art has any relevance for our present unfinished process of becoming human, then we can be sure the author did not flinch from openly connecting his name, the sign of his individuality, with what he did. It is indeed a potent thought that absolutely irrespective of what evidence may ever turn up in an old attic or under ancient floorboards the only valid answer to the authorship question is one of internal artistic integrity. The art itself carries the answer.

Some references by Rudolf Steiner to Shakespeare

In 1910, speaking in Berlin, Rudolf Steiner describes how poetry came from the spiritual world and entered the human ego, at first through the clairvoyant vision of Homer where human beings act out the drama of the gods, and then through Aeschylus, whose Orestes shows the beginnings of an independent man of action. These Greek poets have a sense of the cosmic origins of their inspiration, whereas Dante then finds the source of his inspiration in the depths of his own soul; his revelations of the spiritual world arise within him. Rudolf Steiner then speaks about the next step in this 'descent' in connection with Shakespeare.

> Shakespeare, on the other hand, creates an abundance of all possible characters—a Lear, Hamlet, Cordelia, Desdemona. But we have no direct perception of anything divine behind these characters, when the spiritual eye beholds them in the physical world, with their purely human qualities and impulses. We look only for what comes directly from their souls in the form of thinking, feeling and willing. They are all distinct individuals, but can we recognize Shakespeare himself in them, in the way that Dante is always Dante when he immerses himself in his own personality? No—Shakespeare has taken another step forward. He penetrates still further

Introduction 15

into the personal element, but not only into one personality but into a wide variety of personalities. Shakespeare denies himself whenever he describes Lear, Hamlet and so on; he is never tempted into presenting his own ideas, for as Shakespeare he is completely blotted out; he lives entirely in the various characters he creates. The experiences described by Dante are those of one person; Shakespeare shows us impulses arising from the inner ego in the widest diversity of characters. Dante's starting point is human personality; he remains within it and from there he explores the spiritual world. Shakespeare has gone a step further: he, too, starts from his own personality and slips into the individuals he portrays; he is wholly immersed in them. It is not his own soul-life that he dramatizes, but the lives of the characters in the outer world that he presents on the stage, and they are all depicted as independent persons with their own motives and aims.

Thus we can see here, again, how the evolution of art proceeds. Having originated in the remote past, when human consciousness was devoid of ego-feeling, with Dante art reached the stage of embracing individual man, so that the ego itself became a world. With Shakespeare, it expanded so far that other egos became the poet's world. For this step to be possible, art had to leave the spiritual heights from which it had sprung and descend into the actualities of physical existence. And this is just what we can see happening when we pass on from Dante to Shakespeare.

Starting from the direct spiritual perception of a

higher world, art takes hold of man's inner life to an ever-increasing degree. It does so most intimately when—as with Dante—a man is dealing with himself alone. In Shakespeare's plays the ego goes out from this inwardness and enters other souls.[2]

Rudolf Steiner points here to the fact that Shakespeare's plays are not autobiographical; his own personal life experience is not the source of his inspiration. What he does bring out of his life experience is his practised stagecraft, and he brings together with that a creative genius for language. The plots he borrows and adapts liberally. But the essence of his art, the characters, their actions and interactions, their motives and the effects and consequences of how they act, their development, the evolving individual, interpersonal and social dynamics, all this flows through him from a source that is certainly greater than one man can possibly experience in a lifetime. His great achievement is to hold back the exigencies of his personal biography and allow something universally human to inspire his artistic skills poetically and dramatically. An exploration of the sonnets would reveal something different, but it is not insignificant that we actually know so little about his life.

The frontispiece illustration by Abram Games is a fine artistic expression of this reality: the important things we know about Shakespeare are his works; his artistic achievements make up the face he presents to the world.

Then in 1917, speaking in Dornach, Rudolf Steiner again mentions Shakespeare.[3] He first characterizes how the translations and attitudes of Schlegel and Tieck, Lessing and

Goethe allowed these dramas to be thoroughly assimilated into the stream of German culture, and then amusingly relates that in a lecture he had heard when he came to Vienna Karl Julius Schröer announced he was going to speak about 'the three greatest German poets, Schiller, Goethe and Shakespeare!'

In the same lecture Rudolf Steiner makes a passing but precious allusion to how evolution proceeds by apparent contraries. The rise of materialism in Britain is accompanied by what I understand to be its spiritual-cultural antidote. Beneath the surface of outer events there is a spiritual impulse that seeks to bring about harmony, and he connects this to James I, whose contribution provided a necessary connection to the whole of European culture. Rudolf Steiner states that the same source that inspired Shakespeare also inspired Francis Bacon, the founder of modern materialism, the Jesuit Jakobus Baldus, and Jakob Boehme.

In 1920[4] he expands on this theme, exploring the significance of Bacon's contribution to our modern scientific thinking and reiterating that Bacon and Shakespeare were inspired by the same spiritual source. Although the specific references in this lecture to Shakespeare are not many, it provides relevant and illuminating spiritual-historical background, and we have included it in this publication on pages 27–46. If we understand an aspect of the greater task of materialism as part of the condition in which spiritual science is so deeply longed for today, then this 'brotherliness' between Bacon and Shakespeare will at first maybe surprise us, but not remain a paradox. It becomes grotesque if it leads to authorship confusion, but as an insight into how the spiritual world ensures that culture provides the redemptive forces for the unavoidable experiences of earthly death, it is truly Rosicrucian.

This theme, the significance of James I, and additional references Rudolf Steiner makes to it in *Karmic Relationships*[5] and in a conversation reported by Albert Steffen[6] are extensively examined by Richard Ramsbotham in his masterly research published in the book *Who Wrote Bacon*.[7]

Commentary on lectures Rudolf Steiner gave in 1922

Rudolf Steiner takes up the theme of Hamlet in connection with the wider European context and what he calls 'world spiritual history', specifically in connection with Goethe and Faust. This lecture[8] is reprinted in full on pages 47–66. Rudolf Steiner describes how Goethe was not content to depict the original Faustian figure of the fifteenth and sixteenth century whose intellectual achievements were no longer satisfying, and much as Goethe himself strove to get beyond the confines of what science could say about the human being, Faust aspires to something more. Then Rudolf Steiner posits the idea that Hamlet might have been a student in Wittenberg with a professor much like Faust, and that the central drama in Hamlet's life arises from finding himself between an intellectual book-knowledge and an evident openness to the spiritual world. It is clear for Rudolf Steiner that Shakespeare was writing at a time of transition, a time when the reality of ghosts was still taken for granted and that there was no need to 'explain' whether such phenomena (as also occur in Macbeth) were subjective or objective. In his monologues Hamlet gives expression to the riddles of his age, a twilight condition of transition between a vanishing past and a not-yet fully arrived future, and in Lear this becomes a state of madness. For Rudolf Steiner what characterizes this aspect of Shakespeare is that the dramatist brings to expression this transition out of the past, but then apparently concludes with an acceptance of the conditions of his own time, coming to terms with things as they are in Elizabethan and Jacobean England. These observations about how Shakespeare's dramas culimate and where they end up (on page 59) might strike the reader today as somewhat incomplete. What Shakespeare represents in the later plays, understood in the context of Rudolf Steiner's descriptions of our potential future evolution, offers so much more. What seems to be a lack here is more than compensated for by what Rudolf Steiner said in the third lecture (pages 67–84).

The transitions of this age in every aspect of life in Britain, not least in the development of the English language, are finely observed, and the chaos and madness in Hamlet, Ophelia, Othello, Lady Macbeth and Lear are palpable. In the case of Ophelia, we might be struck by this tension between past and future when in her madness she says:

> Lord, we know what we are, but know not what we may be (Act IV, Scene V)

Never in the prison of her sanity could she have expressed this. There is a kind of weight from the past balanced against an openness for the future, a juxtaposition of guilt and reimagined innocence. When we are 'deranged' the old arrangement of concepts and criteria are shifted; that might sometimes be comical, or dangerous, but it is also sometimes an opening to a new perspective. In his madness, bereft of kingly trappings, Lear can perceive 'unaccommodated man' for the first time, and Ophelia's bereavement prompts a derangement that briefly allows her this precious insight into our unpredictable human destiny.

In a lecture given two days later in the same cycle, Rudolf Steiner recapitulates some of these ideas about Shakespeare.[9] In the following edited extract we are invited to see Hamlet's inability to kill his uncle as stemming from the intellectualized learning he might have been subjected to under a professor such as the old Faust. At this point Rudolf Steiner says nothing about what Shakespeare's contribution to the future might be, but the way he perceives Lear, Hamlet and Macbeth's proximity to the spiritual world is beautifully expressed.

> The character which Shakespeare created out of Hamlet—who in his turn he had taken from Danish mythology and transformed—could have been a pupil of Faust, one of those very students whom Faust had led by the nose 'these ten years long'. We see Hamlet interacting with the spiritual world. His task is given to him by the spiritual world, but he is constantly prevented from fulfilling it by the qualities he has acquired as a result of his intellectual education...
>
> Further, I said that in the whole mood and artistic form of Shakespeare's plays, that is, in the historical plays, we

could find in the creativity of the writer of Shakespeare's plays the twilit mood of that time of transition. Then I drew your attention to the way in which Goethe and Schiller in Central Europe had stood in their whole life of soul within the dying vibrations of the transition, yet had lacked, in a certain sense, the will to accept what the intellectual view of the world had since then brought about in the life of human beings. This led them back to Shakespeare, for in his work—*Hamlet*, *Macbeth* and so on—they discovered the capacity to approach the spiritual world. From his vantage point, they could see into the world of spiritual powers which was now hidden from the intellectual viewpoint...

I indicated further that, in the West, Shakespeare was in a position—if I may put it like this—to work artistically in full harmony with his social environment. *Hamlet* is the play most characteristic of Shakespeare. Here the action is everywhere quite close to the spiritual world, as it is also in *Macbeth*. In *King Lear*, for instance, we see how he brings the supersensible world more into the human personality, into an abnormal form of the human personality, the element of madness. Then, in the historical dramas about the kings, he goes over more into realism but, at the same time, we see in these plays a unique depiction of a long drawn-out dramatic evolution influenced everywhere by the forces of destiny, but culminating and coming to an end in the age of Queen Elizabeth.

The thing that is at work in Shakespeare's plays is a retrospective view of older ages leading up to the time in which he lives, a time which is seen to be accepted by him. Everything belonging to older times is depicted artistically in a way which leads to an understanding of the time in which he lives. You could say that Shakespeare portrays the past. But he portrays it in such a way that he places himself in his contemporary western social environment, which he shows to be a time in which things can take the course which they are prone to take. We see a certain satisfaction with regard to what has come about in the external world. The intellectualism of the social order is accepted by the person belonging to the external, physical earthly world, by the social human being, whereas the artistic human being in Shakespeare goes back to earlier times and portrays that aspect of the supersensible world which has created pure intellectualism.

Then we see that in Central Europe this becomes an impossibility. Goethe and Schiller and before them Lessing cannot place themselves within the social order in a way which enables them to accept it. They all look back to Shakespeare, but to that Shakespeare who himself went back into the past. They want the past to lead to something different from the present time in which they find themselves. Shakespeare is in a way satisfied with his environment; but they are dissatisfied with theirs... Shakespeare in a way brings the supersensible world down into the sense-perceptible world.

The truth of this last sentence becomes even more evident in the last plays. The transition of the experience from dream to reality for Pericles, then for Posthumus (*Cymbeline*) and finally for Leontes (*A Winters Tale*) is indeed a powerful affirmation of exactly what Rudolf Steiner here describes. Leontes awakens from what he thinks is an illusion to discover it is blissfully true, the illusory distinction between vision and reality is dispelled. Shakespeare brings us powerfully down into the sense-perceptible world with a profoundly spiritual event, the reunion after 16 years of a penitent man with his forgiving wife. Then in *The Tempest* we are briefly reminded of the illusions we have left behind, the masque Prospero conjures up has no real substance and is summarily dismissed when more pressing earthly matters arise.

This sequence, culminating in *The Tempest* is indeed an affirmation that it is also here on earth that our spiritual experiences can be real, not in dreamlike states but in full day-consciousness.

In April 1922 Rudolf Steiner was in Stratford-upon-Avon for the Shakespeare Festival and gave two lectures.[10] Although in the first lecture Shakespeare is mentioned at the beginning and at the end, it is principally about education. In the second lecture, given on 23 April, Rudolf Steiner speaks about the timeless power that lives in Shakespeare's work and how modern that is (see p. 68). He derides Goethe's 'barren' intellectual commentaries on Shakespeare, and rejoices at Goethe's spontaneous recognition of the life in Shakespeare's work.

Here in the lecture given in Shakespeare's place of birth and on his birthday we find something that perhaps we had missed in the lectures given two months earlier. After saying how a modern and 'exact clairvoyance' can enable us to understand why it is that the characters in Shakespeare's plays continue to live and breathe beyond the confines of their written roles, Rudolf Steiner describes the experience of the on-going life that flows from what Shakespeare wrote, and the profound spiritual origins of his inspirations. He reminds us of the sources and characteristics of classical Greek drama, he recalls Aristotle's definition of drama as catharsis, and then points to the connection Shakespeare has to these cultural and later historical origins and the development he himself goes through. He concludes with a paean to the universally human qualities that live in Shakespeare and how they can inspire us in our longing for modern ideals.

This lecture is indeed a fitting, concluding celebration for Shakespeare. We have included on pages 85–86 a report Rudolf Steiner himself wrote on his experience of the Festival.[11]

In the German edition of the Speech and Drama Course given in Dornach in September 1924 (GA 282), but not published in the English edition, there are included some answers Rudolf Steiner gave to questions about the dramatic arts in a conversation he had with actors on 10 April 1921. He makes various comments about aspects of Shakespeare, notably that it was with the whole of his own humanness that he could see and portray the whole of the human being. And then he enters into the most imaginative description of the tavern-like theatre of Shakespeare's day with a prescience that beautifully anticipates the dissolution of the old distinctions, which is indeed the culminating quality of *The Tempest*. He describes how the division between stage and auditorium was not rigid, the structure of the stage protruded into the auditorium, there were seats at the side of the stage for certain privileged theatre-goers, actors speaking from the side seemed part of the audience, and the reactions and interactions with the audience were an integral part of the experience. Shakespeare knew well how to enchant the public, the very music of the lines makes clear how he spoke to the people from the heart. Rudolf Steiner also comments, not uncritically, in this section on the prevailing tendency to play Hamlet as a melancholy, philosophical character. He then offers a fairly detailed analysis of the soul moods in the 'to be or not to be' speech (he makes a side remark that some German translations are better than the original English!), and pleads for an interpretation of the role that arises out of a sensitivity to what lives in the words.

Andrew Wolpert

Notes

1. Rudolf Steiner speaks about the supersensible School of Michael in several lectures given between 20 July and 14 September in 1924, GAs 237, 238 and 240, published in volumes 3, 4 and 6 of *Karmic Relationships*, Rudolf Steiner Press.
2. *Transforming the Soul*, Vol. 2, Lecture 9, 'The Mission of Art', Berlin, 12 May 1910. GA 59, Rudolf Steiner Press, 2006.
3. *The Karma of Untruthfulness*, Vol. 2, Lecture 20, Dornach, 15 January 1917, GA 174, Rudolf Steiner Press, 2005.
4. 1 February 1920, GA 196, reprinted in *What is Necessary in These Urgent Times*, SteinerBooks, 2010.
5. *Karmic Relationships*, Vol. 2, 12 April 1924, GA 236, Rudolf Steiner Press, 2015.
6. *Das Goetheanum*, 12 April 1925.
7. Richard Ramsbotham, *Who Wrote Bacon?*, Temple Lodge, 2004.
8. *Old and New Methods of Initiation*, Lecture 11, Dornach, 24 February 1922, GA 210, Rudolf Steiner Press, 1991.
9. Ibid., 26 February 1922, GA 210.
10. *Waldorf Education and Anthroposophy*, Anthroposophic Press, 1995.
11. Ibid., pp. x–xi.

Lecture 1

DORNACH, 1 FEBRUARY 1920

What I have to say today as a further development of my recent lectures will lead us to consider the deeds of individual human beings in history from a specific spiritual-scientific perspective. We are used to thinking of significant individuals in history—be they artistic, political, religious or otherwise—as people whose deeds come out of conscious impulses arising within them, and that this is the sole cause of the actions these people take in the world. And we then consider the questions that arise from this perspective, asking: What did this individual do? What did this individual say? What did this individual bring to other people? And so on.

But in the case of significant historical events, the matter is not nearly so straightforward. What is actively at work in human evolution depends upon the driving spiritual forces that stand behind history's unfolding, and individuals are simply the means and paths through which certain driving spiritual forces reach from the spiritual world into earth's history.

This does not contradict the idea that the individuality, the subjectivity of significant persons, has an effect on the larger circles of the world. Their influence is self-evident. But you will have a true understanding of history only if you clearly see that when a so-called great individual says something or another, in some place or another, the directing spiritual powers of human evolution are speaking through that person, and the individual is only a symptom of the existence of these driving forces. That individual is the doorway through which these forces enter world history.

So if, for example, someone from a particular period of history were to be quoted, and you attempted to characterize the influence of those words on the whole of that time period, then (if you were speaking from a spiritual-scientific perspective) you would not claim that this individual had only practised such influence on the world through the force of his or her personality alone. Let me give you a specific example. Let us assume (as we do in short order) that a particular philosophical man was quoted as being especially characteristic of his time period. Someone else could come along and say: 'Well, this person certainly wrote many philosophical texts, but he only has an influence on certain circles. The vast majority of people were not influenced by this person at all.'

It would be entirely false to reply in such a way, because the individual mentioned, though also a philosophical figure, is simply the expression of certain forces that stand behind him, and these forces then influence and shape other forces in the world. In the individual we see only the expression of what is actively at work in that time period.

For example, the following might be the case. At some point in history, there might be some sort of spiritual stream, some sort of spiritual directive at work in the subconscious circles of human souls. This might then find expression in a particular individual, someone who is able to formulate in an uncommonly clear manner things about which larger circles of people, perhaps even entire populations, had only some small inkling. But this person might never write it down and might talk about it with only five or six other people, or might perhaps not speak about it at all. In this extreme case, it could be that centuries later, the memoirs of such a person were discovered, and in them had been written things that had never been published or distributed. Nevertheless, those memoirs might contain the characteristic ideas and forces at work in that time period.

Whenever I have attempted to describe historical figures, I have always done so from this perspective. I never intended to awaken the belief that an individual's ideas are able to have an effect only when they are administered through the normal lines of propaganda. Rather, I always wanted to demonstrate that we find expressions of the most influential ideas in individual personalities. Of course, accompanying this is the possibility that the important influence of such individuals is not felt during the time in which they are alive. It is, of course, also possible for the exact opposite to be true. Such individuals can have a very large effect on many circles of humanity. But the former point must be made expressly clear so that people do not say to themselves: 'When one describes an individual as influential and significant in a particular time period, one is speaking only about something happening in some small corner of the human world; I am interested in hearing a description of what was going on for humanity as a whole.' I would ask you all to consider all of what I have to say today with this perspective in mind.

I have spoken often about the pronounced leap forward in the historical unfolding of humanity that occurred in the fifteenth century. Anyone who studies the soul-life of civilized human beings will find that soul-life in the sixteenth and seventeenth centuries was radically different than soul-life in the tenth, eleventh and twelfth centuries. I have also often indicated how incorrect it is to say (though it is repeated often): 'The natural world and historical events on earth do not make any "leap".' Such leaps always occur at significant moments in evolution. And one such leap in the evolution of civilized humanity occurred at the transition from the fourth post-Atlantean epoch, which ended in the fifteenth century, to the fifth post-Atlantean epoch, which we are living in currently and which has only just begun. The entire way of thinking, the entire form of civilized European human thought, was different, in a certain sense, after the fifteenth century; but the changes that occurred were different for the people of each nation, for the members of each population. Certain transitional phenomena appeared in the various populations of Europe in different ways.

Now, we cannot understand the spiritual life in which we currently find ourselves if we do not have a perspective on what has developed in our spiritual life since the fifteenth century. We must have an understanding of certain characteristic aspects of this newly emerging spiritual life. As always, it is possible to describe only certain individual streams and perspectives. If you consider the time that immediately preceded this fifth post-Atlantean epoch, from the Mystery of Golgotha through to the fifteenth century, you would have to say: 'During this time, a large number of people in civilized Europe were attempting to gain an understanding, a religious understanding, of Christianity.'

Anyone who makes the effort to study the individual perspectives on Christianity that appeared in Europe from the third and fourth centuries through to the fifteenth century will find that the people of civilized Europe used all of their thinking and feeling capacities, everything they could draw up out of their souls, to understand Christianity in their own way, to gain some understanding of their own about what the world had become through the Mystery of Golgotha.

After the turn of the fifteenth century, a set of very special circumstances came about. The first of these—and for those who do not pay any regard to that tall tale typically referred to as 'history', but rather pay attention to true history, all of this is entirely clear—was the emergence of what people almost everywhere refer to as scientific thinking. Before then, something altogether different was present. What is seen today as truly scientific had its beginning at the start of the fifth post-Atlantean epoch. And it was expressed with a very particular structure, and one might say it was expressed in several different ways. Actually, what was expressed was always the same, but it received a different minting in the West, in western civilization, than it received in Central European civilization. And now the time has come in which these matters must be considered freely, without the influence of nationalistic ideas (in the negative sense that I described yesterday).

And should we want to consider a representative individual living at this time in which a new age was given its spiritual signature, we immediately come upon one especially characteristic of the transition from the sixteenth into the seventeenth century—the English philosopher Francis

Bacon of Verulam. Among those who consider themselves scientific, Bacon is seen as someone who revolutionized our way of thinking. But Bacon is a by-product, a symptom of something that was entering history in this new age, as I have just described. In essence, a wave of new thinking completely washed over the western world, and Bacon is merely the individual who expressed it in the western world most clearly. Though we are not aware of it, this wave of new thinking lives in each one of us. The way we think in the western world, the way we express ourselves regarding the most important matters in life, is 'Baconian', even when people dispute Bacon's points, even when we argue against something he said. It does not have much to do with the content of what we say when offering ideas about a way of seeing the world; it has more to do first with how such ideas reach into the human heart, and then how they integrate into the impulses of the world's historical unfolding.

To make what I have just said clearer, we can cite the following paradox. In these times, one person might be a full-blown materialist and another a full-blown spiritualist, and yet both might very well speak out of the perspective of our materialistic times—there might be no great difference between the two. It does not matter nowadays whether the literal content of someone's words tends toward materialism or spiritualism. What matters is the spirit out of which one practises one perspective or the other. For what actually has an effect in the world is not the literal content of something, but the spirit out of which it comes. That is what has an impact. Only if you are an abstraction yourself will you offer anything to the world solely through the literal content of your words.

Now we must note that Bacon—if you examine the spirit out of which his thinking comes—attempted to give a foundation to human knowledge, to science, using spiritual forces that had started to appear in the middle of the fifteenth century. The forces of knowledge placed at the disposal of human beings in this new age were to become the foundation for science. It was an important time, the beginning of the fifth post-Atlantean epoch, when Bacon came to earth. It was, so to speak, the time in which everything was called into question, for people could no longer develop ideas about the riddles of the world by working with alchemy, astrology and other old methods, including old religious ways of thinking. There was a drive towards renewal. In what was the presence of this drive made most evident? This drive was evidenced in the fact that this time period was a low point for all truly spiritual forces of human understanding.

Until the fifteenth century, it would have seemed impossible to try to grasp something like the Mystery of Golgotha with a purely sense-oriented understanding. It was actually held as self-evident that something like the Mystery of Golgotha had to be understood as a phenomenon of the highest sort, to be grasped with higher forces of knowing than those used to understand the natural world that is spread out around us. These higher forces of knowing still had a certain elevated place at the time of the Mystery of Golgotha. As human evolution progressed, they sank ever lower in human consciousness. And as this new age began at the turn of the fifteenth century, people no longer had any spiritual forces of understanding—they only had a sense-oriented understanding of the world.

With this sense-oriented understanding, Bacon sought to provide a foundation for scientific thinking. Consequently, he rejected all of the research methods that had been recognized as legitimate up to that point and held up experimentation as the sole means by which to build up the body of scientific knowledge. A large majority of the world is still in this place: we must experiment, we must construct devices and perform experiments, and these experiments must then provide us with our views about the nature of the world.

From a spiritual perspective, this translates to the following: Here I have a butterfly; it is too complicated for me to examine this butterfly, so I will meticulously construct a model of it out of papier mâché and then examine the model. This is essentially the same as observing living nature through dead experiments, which is no different than replacing a natural living phenomenon with a corpse in the interest of observing the natural phenomenon. Even when we are working in a physics laboratory, we should be aware that we are experimenting on the corpses of natural phenomena. Of course, it is important to conduct experiments, and even to examine human corpses. But when examining a corpse you can have no illusion that it is merely a corpse lying before you. Yet when conducting experiments, we give in to the illusion that they are communicating living truths to us. If you do not already possess the spiritual intuition that allows you to pour into the experiment something of what it is about from out of the living natural world, you will not walk away

Lecture 1   35

from that experiment, that dead experiment, with any truths about the living natural world.

This would indicate that the way of thinking Bacon introduced was intended from the start to make death the basic principle used to explain the world's being. Now, the peculiar thing is that in the reproductions of the living world achieved through experimentation one does discover clues about the non-human world. But we must not delude ourselves into believing that any indications about human beings can be won through experimentation. All experimentation leads away from the being of humankind.

Thus it has come about that in the intervening centuries, during which that way of thinking so highly developed by Bacon was spread throughout the world, any understanding of the human being and its essential nature, of that driving, active being that exists in the human being's inmost core, was lost.

Now, great moral and social will impulses cannot be found without turning towards that essential human nature. As a direct result of Baconian thinking, our understanding of these social and moral will impulses has disappeared during the past few centuries. Consequently, and paralleling the death of our understanding of the world as a result of Bacon's thinking, arose the morality of usefulness. It is a perfectly Baconian definition of morality: a thing is good if it is useful to human beings, either individually or collectively.

So, as a result of Bacon's thinking—and this was far more pervasive than anyone today can truly imagine—we have a scientific system of thought able to understand only the non-human world on the one hand and a morality based on ahrimanic usefulness on the other. The latter found fuller expression in Thomas Hobbes—a contemporary of Bacon—than it did in Bacon himself. But this sweeping morality of usefulness then became the basis for understanding all of the external, non-human world. It washed over all of philosophy from Locke and Hume to Spencer, to the natural scientists from Newton to Darwin. Anyone wanting to study the most characteristic parts of what came out of the western world from its beginnings through to the development of the most recent systems of European thought must begin by studying Baconian thinking.

Now, something very important is also connected with the Baconian system of thought and morality. It only allows you to examine the non-human world, only allows you to think over morality in terms of what is useful to humans and humankind. This means that by using this system's methods of scientific and moral pursuit you can achieve nothing in the realm of religion!

What was the consequence of this? As a result, the bearers of this system of thought strove to leave religion as it had been, to preserve and propagate it historically, not to offer it any new elements out of a new science of spirit. Bacon himself defended the most characteristic perspective, that science was not to be brought together with religion, for the connection would cause science to become fantastic; and religion was not to be brought together with science, for the connection would turn religion into heterodoxy.

And so religion was held at a comfortable distance from scientific pursuits. The new forces active in civilized humankind since the fifteenth century were directed towards scientific pursuits. None of these new forces were directed towards religion. Religion was to be preserved by the forces that had been directed towards it in the past, for people feared the new forces that might be directed towards it. They feared that it would become heterodoxy, that it would lose its true content.

What was the only thing that could have resulted from the influence of such a system of thought? What actually happened? People strove with a certain truthfulness after science and knowledge of the physical world, strove out of that same truthfulness after a morality of usefulness, but they did not want to strive after religion in the same way they strove after science. Religion was not to be touched. It was not to receive any consideration from this genuine scientific striving. At most, religion was to be studied historically.

This is what led to the difference between science and organized religion. This difference can also be explained in stronger language. It can be explained as follows (which is simply a stronger way of putting it, but this makes it more uncomfortable for those who do not like to hear the truth). It can be characterized as follows. People strive genuinely after science—namely a science that reaches out to the physical world. People also strive just as genuinely and earnestly after usefulness. But they do not turn this genuine striving towards religion, for religion must remain unsullied; science may not touch it. Genuine physical science, genuine drive for usefulness—religion as hypocrisy, religion taken from untruthfulness: this is just a stronger way of putting it, and is consequently more discomfiting for those who do not care to hear the uncensored truth about the difference between science and organized religion. But in speaking in such a strong and definite manner, one arrives at the heart of the matter. And what I have said is truly the defining character of this way of thinking, in which one recoils from the application of science to religion, in which it is not desirable for a science engaged in the study of nature and the like to play a role in religion.

For the most part, this way of thinking came naturally to western civilization. It exists so naturally as a part of it that countless people in western civilization do not understand that it could be any other way—one simply does not apply natural-scientific principles to religion. This is characteristic of the western world. It is entirely fitting.

But now, let us imagine the same impulse shipped over into Central Europe. I can offer you the following representative example. It does not always happen that this system of thought meets an opposition as sharp as the one Newtonian thinking encountered in Goethe. Rather, something like Darwinism, which is oriented only towards the physical body and cannot result in anything other than a morality of usefulness, is taken up by an ancient Central European, we might even say Prussian Central European man, such as Ernst Haeckel. Here, things are a little different than they were in the case of Darwin. In Darwin, we see Bacon's thinking carried forward and developed. Darwin regards the natural world through his own Darwinian lens, but he continues to be a believer, just as Newton did. He quietly preserves in himself an old way of thinking in regard to purely religious matters.

Now what about Haeckel? Haeckel takes Darwinism

completely into his soul. For him, there is no possibility of dividing his thinking into two parts. For him, there is no possibility of leaving religion untouched. He takes Darwinism, which one can really use to understand only the non-human world, and then, with religious fervour, he turns its gaze towards the human world and makes a religion out of it. The two parts become one. A religion results from this union.

And in this way, an impulse existing in one place has an effect all over. The impulse remains the same, but it works in different ways, specific to the various regions of the world. In the West, people effectively hold religion and Darwinism separate from one another, bearing them through the course of world evolution. Ernst Haeckel, the Central European, mixes the two together and serves up a single dish, because for him it simply does not work to hold the two next to one another, but separate. Bacon and his followers, through Spencer and Darwin, feared that religion would become heterodoxy if one were to turn science towards it. Haeckel did not have the same fear. He did the best he could with religion, for he took the same truthfulness used in pursuit of science and brought it to bear on his religious views.

The same is true in many areas. Even the Goetheanism in Goethe inwardly opposed an understanding solely of the non-human world. You need only read the prose-hymn 'Nature', which Goethe had at least thought of in the '80s, even if he had not written it down at that time (and which has been performed here as a eurythmy piece), and you will see that Goethe does not think of nature in the same way as Newton or Darwin. Rather, he sees it as inwardly ensouled.

There is even some humour in it: '...It has thought, and is thinking still.' And throughout his life, Goethe developed ever more concrete forms of these kinds of maxims, which he wrote down in his *Fragments* on nature.

Recently, an article appeared in a paper here—a continuation of it appeared in this Sunday's paper, I believe—that said that when I published the 'Fragment' on nature along with a commentary, in a new edition of the *Tiefurter Journal* in the papers of the Weimar Goethe Society back in the '90s, I had emphasized too strongly that the details that Goethe was working through in the prose-hymn 'Nature' went on to play a role in his work in natural science. It is strange, the objection raised in this article. It said that there are no natural philosophical ideas in this 'Fragment' but rather religious ones, and that one may not connect the religious ideas in this prose-hymn with the later natural philosophical works of Goethe, as I had done. So a pedant (for what else might we call him) has the satisfaction of splitting all those seeking some understanding of humanity in two by telling them that the natural-scientific ideas of Goethe are different from the religious ideas. From the very start, this conclusion was drawn in a manner that makes it clear that Baconian thinking lies behind everything this man says.

Can we now—I would like to post the question this way—also see another way in which religion and science are differentiated in modern civilization? We can indeed. Certainly, even in England, the land of Bacon, there were men such as Wycliffe and others like him; but this did not have an influence on the actual structures of civilization. In Central Europe, on the other hand, something occurred that had a major effect upon civilization, but whose influence did not reach into the West—for example, into France. As the new era began, this fifth post-Atlantean epoch, there was no opposition in Central Europe of the sort that occurred in the West, where science was properly founded but not allowed to affect religious concerns, which were to continue in perpetuity as they had up to that point in the old forms of organized religion. In Central Europe, the opposition was instead taken up strongly in the form of the Reformation, and this resulted in that unfortunate event in Central European evolution, the inciting of the Thirty Years' War by the Jesuits, as well as everything that happened because of that war, and everything that followed after that as well. Here we see an example of how the impulse that had arisen during the fifteenth century became active in religious concerns in Central Europe.

In the smallest and in the most significant historical events, we can see that this same impulse is always there, but it is always slightly askew, drawn up out of the particularities of a certain population, of certain individuals. But again and again it is the western world that leads the way forward, and again and again something significant occurs. The farther we look into the future development of the spiritual life in Central Europe in the time since Goethe, the farther we see it moving away from Goethe. Goethe will continue to be studied by the literary historians and others, of course. After all, there is even a Goethe Institute. But Goethe is not present in any of those things. What Goethe actually intended to bring as an impulse into Central European civilization—Goethe and his followers—that impulse sickened gradually during the nineteenth century. And in the

Central European world, just as Darwinism gave way to Haeckelism, all of the impulses coming out of the western world have also gradually sickened. The western world bears these impulses well, but the Central European world does not.

On the one hand, we have Darwin, who, in his final work, using principles that are applicable only to the non-human world, gave some indications of the significance that his work might have for humans, but these indications were nowhere near as wide-reaching as the ones that Haeckel later worked on. In Darwin's case, the principles of science were applied primarily to the non-human world. In Central Europe, on the other hand, everything went the way that Haeckelism went in relation to Darwinism: people tried to fill their entire lives with impulses such as this one. They would not hold apart certain (for example religious) aspects of their lives; they attempted to push these impulses into those areas as well. And the same is true of other, similarly distinct areas of life.

Those who are older now actually experienced this when the parliamentarianism of England spread throughout all of Europe, with the exception of Prussian Germany, and was taken up just as Darwinism was taken up in Haeckelism. Parliamentarianism, as it existed in England, was a good fit for England. For the countries of Central Europe into which it has been transplanted, it is bound up with the same set of consequences that accompany Haeckel and Darwinism. The modern age arose under the influence of these things.

But we can go deeper still and characterize these historical occurrences in a deeper way. In addition to Bacon, there is another tremendous influence on the modern age in the personage of Shakespeare. For those who are in a position to study spiritual life, to speak of Bacon and of Shakespeare is to allude to the same more-than-earthly source, which is then represented in the earthly—both took the same path into recent evolution, and it is known in spiritual circles that the inspiration for Bacon and for Shakespeare came from the same source. In recent times, where everything has become crude, this has even lead some to posit the well-known 'Bacon Theory', which, naturally, as it has been proposed, is complete nonsense.

But out of the very same fount from which Bacon and Shakespeare drew their inspiration—indeed, stemming from the same initiated persons—came the spiritual stream of Jakob Boehme and the southern German Jakobus Baldus into Central Europe. And all that came from Jakob Boehme is much more alive in Central European spiritual life than is commonly believed—here, again, we have a person who gave a form to something that worked its way as fact into the widest of circles, even if it was not expressed there in Jakob Boehme's words. We must understand clearly that a good portion of Goethe's teachings on metamorphosis can be traced back to Jakob Boehme, that a good portion of Goethe's whole organic chemistry came to him from Jakob Boehme via certain detours and circuitous routes that can also be easily traced backwards. And even though Jakobus Baldus lived in sleepy little Ingolstadt, he too is one of those individuals who, though he did not have a big effect on his contemporaries, gave expression in a very characteristic way to certain things that were felt and thought in the widest of circles in this newly begun epoch.

But let us consider the strange depths of these matters: Bacon and Shakespeare, Boehme, Baldus—all came from the same source of inspiration. What came from Jakob Boehme can still be seen at the core of Central Europe's strivings, but it has grown sick. In its place, Baconian thinking, whether itself or in the form of the later Darwinism, has taken on a position of significant influence in Central Europe. Shakespeare has taken on a similar position of influence. Consider the fact that the entire second half of the eighteenth century (or at the very least the later portion of it) was influenced by Shakespeare; that nineteenth-century spiritual life in Central Europe was heavily influenced by him; that Goethe, in his youth, was deeply influenced by him and only freed himself from Shakespeareanism in the '80s.

Everywhere, we can detect the same paths. Everywhere, the impulses are the same. But they work in different ways. In Central Europe, the impulses sickened over time. The western impulses washed over the non-human world. They made religious life into a life of hypocrisy existing next to and apart from scientific pursuits. And as these western elements have flooded into the whole of modern civilization, we see that people even today have not arrived at a point where they can direct these spiritual powers—the spiritual science stemming from human nature itself that must take hold in modern times, just as the scientific powers directed at the non-human world have done—towards religious life. It is time for a new understanding of Christianity, because nothing further can be done with all that has been left untouched thus far—it is time to work on a new understanding, with new spiritual powers. The old spiritual powers are used up, and those who believe today that they are at all able to understand Christianity with the old spiritual powers that have been recognized as belonging to religious life—they live in a terrible illusion. It must be said that a new epoch of humanity, in which the Mystery of Golgotha itself will be understood with new spiritual powers, must come. For everything that has been said about it has outlived its truth and usefulness. It has reached the point of absurdity. It can be pieced together here and there, taken up now and again in such a way that people can treat it as something insignificant, a sort of scientific 'doesn't-bother-me-at-all'—but humanity cannot live any longer with these things. Humanity needs the strength to draw out from within itself the new spiritual powers that will allow it to understand the Mystery of Golgotha in a new way.

This is what the people of the western world have seen—that it is incumbent upon them to look through the lens of these new spiritual powers. For in this western world people have limited themselves to a simple understanding of the non-human world. This knowledge of the non-human world will never be applicable to the human world. People will have to come to an understanding of a new spiritual science, which will first offer a new outlook on the Mystery of Golgotha. What concerns only the non-human world can simply give rise to a morality of usefulness, but this morality will never bring humanity to the heights of its existence. The only thing that will help it achieve this grandeur is a morality that we know shapes us through supersensory powers at work in our souls. Such a morality, however, can never be understood by what little has been left to religious revelation in the western world. Hence, the need for renewal.

The questions that I have touched upon here may seem to lie far, far above and beyond all aspects of everyday life, but this is not the case. These questions are the most important, world-shaping questions before us right now, and no one will be able to answer the great question 'Where do East and West stand?' 'Where do Europe, Asia, and America stand?' unless we are willing to consider these matters. For when all is said and done, what we are experiencing today are the consequences of everything that has happened in human souls throughout the course of the previous centuries.

Because people are comfortable thinking in the way they do presently, they do not want to consider these matters. And consequently, we can experience what I will call a terrible heartache, which overcomes us when we hear people nowadays speak about the great misfortunes of these times, about the various structures of contemporary politics or economic life or something of the sort, about the situation in Asia, Europe or the Americas—it is like listening to the blind discussing colour, because these people will not direct their gaze towards what lies at the very heart of these great questions.

Lecture 2

DORNACH, 24 FEBRUARY 1922

The turning point, between the fourth and fifth post-Atlantean periods, which falls in the fifteenth century, is very much more significant for human evolution than is recognized by external history, even today. There is no awareness of the tremendous change which took place at that time in the condition of human souls. We can say that profound traces of what took place at that time for mankind as a whole became deeply embedded in the consciousness of the best spirits. These traces remained for a long time and are indeed still there today. That something so important can take place without at first being much noticed externally is shown by another example—that of Christianity itself.

During the course of almost two thousand years, Christianity has wrought tremendous transformation on the civilized world. Yet, a century after the Mystery of Golgotha, it meant little, even to the greatest spirits of the leading culture of the time—that of Rome. It was still seen as a minor event of little significance that had taken place out there in Asia, on the periphery of the Empire. Similarly, what took place in the civilized world around the first third of the fifteenth century has been little noted in external, recorded history. Yet it has left deep traces in human striving and endeavour.

We spoke about some aspects recently. For instance, we saw that Calderón's drama about the magician Cyprianus shows how this spiritual change was experienced in Spain. Now it is becoming obvious—though it is not expressed in the way anthroposophy has to express it—that in all sorts of places at this point in human evolution there is a more vital sense for the need to gain greater clarity of soul about this change. I have also pointed out that Goethe's *Faust* is one of the endeavours, one of the human struggles, to gain clarity about it. More light can perhaps be thrown on this *Faust* of Goethe when it is seen in a wider cultural context. But first let us look at Faust himself as an isolated individual.

First of all in his youthful endeavours, stimulated of course by the cultural situation in Europe at that time, Goethe came to depict in dramatic form the striving of human beings in the newly dawning age of the intellect. From the way in which he came across the medieval Faust figure in a popular play or something similar, he came to see him as a representative of all those seeking personalities who lived at that time. Faust belongs to the sixteenth, not the fifteenth century, but of course the spiritual change did not take place in the space of only a year or even a century. It came about gradually over centuries. So the Faust figure came towards Goethe like a personality living in the midst of this seeking and striving that had come from earlier times and would go on into later centuries. We can see that the special nature of this seeking and striving, as it changed from the fourth to the fifth post-Atlantean period, is perfectly clear to Goethe. First he presents Faust as the scholar who is familiar with all four academic faculties. All four faculties have worked on his soul, so that he has taken into his soul the impulses which derive from intellectualism, from intellectualistic science. At the same time he senses how unsatisfying it is for human beings to remain stuck in one-sided intellectualism. As you know, Faust turns away from this intellectualism and, in his own way, towards the practice of magic. Let us be clear about what is meant in this case. What he has gone through by way of 'Philosophy and Jurisprudence, Medicine and even, alas, Theology', is what anyone can go through by studying the intellectualized sciences. It leaves a feeling of dissatisfaction. It leaves behind this feeling of dissatisfaction because anything abstract—and abstraction is the language of these sciences—makes demands only on a part of the human being, the head part, while all the rest is left out of account.

Compare this with what it was like in earlier times. The fact that things were different in earlier times is habitually overlooked. In those earlier times the people who wanted to push forward to a knowledge of life and the world did not turn to intellectual concepts. All their efforts were concentrated on seeing spiritual realities, spiritual beings, behind the sense-perceptible objects of their environment. This is what people find so difficult to understand. In the tenth, eleventh, twelfth centuries those who strove for knowledge did not only seek intellectual concepts. They sought spiritual beings and realities, in accordance with what can be perceived behind sense-perceptible phenomena and not in accordance with what can be merely thought about sense-perceptible phenomena.

This is what constitutes that great spiritual change. What people sought in earlier times was banished to the realm of superstition, and the inclination to seek for real spiritual beings was lost. Instead, intellectual concepts came to be the only acceptable thing, the only really scientific knowledge. But no matter how logically people told themselves that the only concepts and ideas free of any superstition are those which the intellect forms on the basis of sense-perceptible reality, nevertheless these concepts and ideas failed, in the long run, to satisfy the human being as a whole, and especially the human heart and soul. In this way Goethe's Faust finds himself to be so dissatisfied with the intellectual knowledge he possesses that he turns back to what he remembers of the realm of magic.

This was a true and genuine mood of soul in Goethe. He, too, had explored the sciences at the University of Leipzig. Turning away from the intellectualism he met in Leipzig, he started to explore what in *Faust* he later called 'magic', for instance, together with Susanne von Klettenberg and also by studying the relevant books. Not until he met Herder in Strasbourg did he discover a real deepening of vision. In him he found a spirit who was equally averse to intellectualism. Herder was certainly not an intellectual, hence his anti-Kant attitude. He led Goethe beyond what—in a genuinely Faustian mood—he had been endeavouring to discover in connection with ancient magic.

Thus Goethe looked at this Faust of the sixteenth century, or rather at that scholar of the fifteenth century who was growing beyond magic, even though he was still half-immersed in it. Goethe wanted to depict his own deepest inner search, a search which was in him because the traces of the spiritual change from the fourth to the fifth post-Atlantean period were still working in him.

It is one of the most interesting phenomena of recent

cultural evolution that Goethe, who wanted to give expression to his own youthful striving, should turn to that professor from the fifteenth and sixteenth centuries. In the figure of this professor he depicted his own inner soul life and experience. Du Bois-Reymond, of course, totally misunderstood both what lived in Goethe and what lived in the great change that took place in the fifteenth and sixteenth centuries, when he said: Goethe made a big mistake in depicting Faust as he did; he should have done it quite differently. It is right that Faust should be dissatisfied with what tradition had to offer him; but if Goethe had depicted him properly he would have shown, after the early scenes, how he first made an honest woman of Gretchen by marrying her, and then became a well-known professor who went on to invent the electrostatic machine and the air pump. This is what Du Bois-Reymond thought should have become of Faust.

Well, Goethe did not let this happen to Faust, and I am not sure whether it would have been any more interesting if he had done what Du Bois-Reymond thought he should have done. But as it is, Goethe's Faust is one of the most interesting phenomena of recent cultural history because Goethe felt the urge to let this professor from the fifteenth and sixteenth centuries stand as the representative of what still vibrated in his own being as an echo of that spiritual change which came about during the transition from the fourth to the fifth post-Atlantean period.

The sixteenth-century Faust—that is the legendary Faust, not the one who ought to have become the inventor of the electrostatic machine and the air pump—takes up magic and perishes, goes to the devil. We know that this sixteenth-century Faust could not be seen by either Lessing or Goethe as the Faust of the eighteenth century. Now it was necessary to endeavour to show that once again there was a striving for the spirit and that man ought to find his way to salvation, if I may use this expression.

Here, to begin with, is Faust, the professor in the fifteenth and sixteenth centuries. Goethe has depicted him strikingly well, for this is just what such personalities were like at the universities of that time. Of course, the Faust of legend would not have been suitable, for he would have been more like a roaming vagabond Gipsy. Goethe is describing not the legendary Faust but the figure of a professor. Of course, at the profoundest soul level he is an individual, a unique personality. But Goethe does also depict him as a type, as a typical professor of philosophy, or perhaps of medicine, of the fourteenth or fifteenth century. On the one hand he stands in the midst of the culture of his day, occupying himself with the intellectual sciences, but on the other he is not unfamiliar with occult things, which in Goethe's own day were considered nothing more than superstition.

Let us now look at Goethe's Faust in a wider world context. We do make the acquaintance of his famulus and Goethe shows us the relationship between the two. We also meet a student—though judging by his later development he does not seem to have been much influenced by the professor. But apart from this, Goethe does not show us much of the real influence exercised by Faust, in his deeper soul aspects, as he might have taught as a professor in, say, Wittenberg. However, there does exist a pupil of Faust who can lead us more profoundly into this wider world context. There is a pupil of Faust who occupies a place in the cultural history of mankind which is almost equal to that of Professor Faust himself—I am speaking only of Faust as Goethe portrayed him. And this pupil is none other than Hamlet.

Hamlet can indeed be seen as a genuine pupil of Faust. It is not a question of the historical aspect of Faust as depicted by Goethe. The whole action of the drama shows that although the cultural attitudes are those of the eighteenth century, nevertheless Goethe's endeavour was to place Faust in an earlier age. But from a certain point of view it is definitely possible to say: Hamlet, who has studied at Wittenberg and has brought home with him a certain mood of spirit—Hamlet as depicted by Shakespeare, can be seen in the context of world spiritual history as a pupil of Faust. It may even be true to say that Hamlet is a far more genuine pupil of Faust than are the students depicted in Goethe's drama.

Consider the whole character of Hamlet and combine this with the fact that he studied in Wittenberg where he could easily have heard a professor such as Faust. Consider the manner in which he is given his task. His father's ghost appears to him. He is in contact with the real spiritual world. He is really within it. But he has studied in Wittenberg where he was such a good student that he has come to regard the human brain as a book. You remember the scene when Hamlet speaks of the 'book and volume' of his brain. He has studied human sciences so thoroughly that he speaks of writing what he wants to remember on the table of his memory, almost as though he had known the phrase which Goethe would use later when composing his Faust drama:

'For what one has, in black and white, one carries home and then goes through it.' Hamlet is on the one hand an excellent student of the intellectualism taught him at Wittenberg, but on the other hand he is immersed in a spiritual reality. Both impulses work in his soul. The whole of the Hamlet drama stands under the influence of these two impulses. Hamlet—both the drama and the character—stands under the influence of these impulses because, when it comes down to it, the writer of *Hamlet* does not really know how to combine the spiritual world with the intellectual mood of soul. Poetic works which contain characteristics that are so deeply rooted in life provide rich opportunities for discussion. That is why so many books are written about such works, books which do not really make much sense because there is no need for them to make sense. The commentators are constantly concerned with what they consider to be a most important question: Is the ghost in *Hamlet* merely a picture, or does it have objective significance? What can be concluded from the fact that only Hamlet, and not the other characters present on the stage, can see the ghost?

Think of all the learned and interesting things that have been written about this! But of course none of it is connected with what concerned the poet who wrote *Hamlet*. He belonged to the sixteenth and seventeenth centuries. And writing out of the life of that time he could do no other than approach these things in a way which cannot be fixed in abstract concepts. That is why I say that it is not necessary to make any sense of all the various commentaries. We are talking about a time of transition. Earlier, it was quite clear that spiritual beings were as real as tables and chairs, or as a dog or a cat. Although Calderón lived even later than Shakespeare, he still held to this older view. It would not have occurred to him even to hint that the spiritual beings in his works might be merely subjective in character. Because his whole soul was still open to spiritual insight, he portrayed anything spiritual as something just as concrete as dogs and cats.

Shakespeare, whose mood of soul belonged fully to the time of transition, did not feel the need to handle the matter in any other way than that which stated: It might be *like this* or it might be *like that*. There is no longer a clear distinction between whether the spiritual beings are subjective or objective. This is a question which is just as irrelevant for a higher world-view as it would be to ask in real life—not in astronomy, of course—where to draw the line between day and night. The question as to whether one is subjective and the other objective becomes irrelevant as soon as we recognize the objectivity of the inner world of man and the subjectivity of the external world. In *Hamlet* and also, say, in *Macbeth*, Shakespeare maintains a living suspension between the two. So we see that Shakespeare's dramas are drawn from the transition between the fourth and fifth post-Atlantean periods.

The expression of this is clearest in *Hamlet*. It may not be historical but it is none the less true to suggest that perhaps Hamlet was at Wittenberg just at the time when Faust was lecturing not so much about the occult as about the intellectual sciences—from what we said earlier you now know what I mean. Perhaps he was at Wittenberg before Faust admitted to himself that 'straight or crosswise, wrong or right' he had been leading his scholars by the nose these ten years long. Perhaps Hamlet had been at Wittenberg during those very ten years, among those whom Faust had been leading by the nose. We can be sure that during those ten years Faust was not sure of where he stood. So having taken all this in from a soul that was itself uncertain, Hamlet returns and is faced on the one hand with what remains from an earlier age and what he himself can still perceive, and on the other with a human attitude which simply drives the spirits away. Just as ghosts flee before the light, so does the perception of spiritual beings flee before intellectualism. Spiritual vision cannot tolerate intellectualism because the outcome of it is a mood of soul in which the human being is inwardly torn right away from any connection with the spirit. The pallor of thoughts makes him ill in his inner being, and the consequence of this is the soul mood characteristic of the time from the eleventh to the fifteenth centuries and on into even later times. Goethe, who was sensitive to all these things, also had a mood of soul that reached back into this period. We ought to be clear about this.

Take Greek drama. It is unthinkable without the spiritual beings who stand behind it. It is they who determine human destinies. Human beings are woven into the fabric of destiny by the spiritual forces. This fabric brings into ordinary life what human beings would otherwise only experience if they were able consciously to go into the state of sleep. The will impulses which human beings sleep through in their daytime consciousness are brought into ordinary life. Greek destiny is an insight into what man otherwise sleeps through. When the ancient Greek brings his will to bear, when he acts, he is aware that this is not only the working of his daytime consciousness with its insipid thoughts. Because his whole being is at work, he knows that what pulses through him when he sleeps is also at work. And out of this awareness he gains a certain definite attitude to the question of death, the question of immortality.

Now we come to the period I have been describing, in which human beings no longer had any awareness that something spiritual played in—also in their will—while they slept. We come to the period in which human beings thought their sleep was their own, though at the same time they knew from tradition that they have some connection with the spiritual world. Abstract concepts such as 'philosophy, jurisprudence, medicine, and even, alas! theology' begin to take on a shadowy outline of what they will become in modern times. They begin to appear, but at the same time the earlier vision still plays in. This brings about a twilight consciousness. People really did live in this twilight consciousness. Such figures as Faust are, indeed, born out of a twilight consciousness, out of a glance into the spiritual world which resembles a looking over one's shoulder in a dream. Think of the mood behind such words as 'sleep' or 'dream' in *Hamlet*. We can well say that when Hamlet speaks his monologues he is simply speaking about what he senses to be the riddle of his age; he is speaking not theoretically but out of what he actually senses.

So, spanning the centuries and yet connected in spirit, we see that Shakespeare depicts the student and Goethe the professor. Goethe depicted the professor simply because a few more centuries had passed and it was therefore necessary in his time to go further back to the source of what it was all about. Something lived in the consciousness of human beings, something that made the outstanding spirits say: I must bring to expression this state of transition that exists in human evolution.

It is extremely interesting to expand on this world situation still further, because out of it there arise a multitude of all-embracing questions and riddles about life and the world. It is interesting to note, for instance, that amongst the works of Shakespeare *Hamlet* is the one which depicts in its purest form a personality belonging to the whole twilight condition of the transition—especially in the monologues. The way Hamlet was understood in the seventeenth and eighteenth centuries could have led to the question: Where was the stimulus for what exists in Hamlet's soul? The answer points to Wittenberg, the Faust source. Similar questions arise in connection with *Macbeth*. But in *King Lear* we move into the human realm. The question of the spiritual world is not so much concerned with the earth as with the human being—it enters into the human being and becomes a subjective state of mind which leads to madness.

Then Shakespeare's other dramas could also be considered. We could say: What the poet learnt by taking these human characters and leading them to the spiritual realm lives on in the historical dramas about the kings. He does not follow this specific theme in the historical dramas, but the indeterminate forces work on. Taking Shakespeare's dramas all together, one gains the impression that they all culminate in the age of Queen Elizabeth. Shakespeare wanted to depict something that leads from the subconscious, bubbling forces of his people to the intellectual clarity that has especially shone forth from that corner of the civilized world since the age of Elizabeth. From this point of view the whole world of Shakespeare's dramas appears—not perhaps quite like a play with a satisfactory ending, but at least like a drama which does lead to a fairly satisfying conclusion. That is, it leads to a world which then continues to evolve. After the transition had been going on for some time, the dramas lead to Shakespeare's immediate present, which is a world with which it is possible to come to terms. This is the remarkable thing: the world of Shakespeare's dramas culminates in the age in which Shakespeare lived; this is an age with which it is possible to come to terms, because from then on history takes a satisfactory course and runs on into intellectualism. Intellectualism came from the part of the earth out of which Shakespeare wrote; and he depicted this by ending up at this point.

The questions with which I am concerned find their answers when we follow the lines which lead from the pupil Hamlet to the professor Faust, and then ask how it was with Goethe at the time when, out of his inner struggles, he came to the figure of Faust. You see, he also wrote *Götz von Berlichingen*. In *Götz von Berlichingen*, again taken from folk myth, there is a similar confrontation. On the one side you have the old forces of the pre-intellectual age, the old German empire, which cannot be compared with what became the later German empire. You have the knights and the peasants belonging to the pre-intellectual age when the pallor of thoughts did not make human beings ill—when indeed very little was guided from the head, but when the hands were used to such an extent that even an iron hand was needed. Goethe refers back to something that once lived in more recent civilization but which, by its very nature, had its roots in the fourth post-Atlantean period. Over against all this you have in the figure of Weislingen the new element which is developing, the age of intellectualism, which is intimately linked to the way the German princes and their principalities evolved, a development which led eventually to the later situation in Central Europe right up to the present catastrophe.

We see that in *Götz von Berlichingen* Goethe is attacking this system of princes and looking back to times which preceded the age of intellectualism. He takes the side of the old and rebels against what has taken its place, especially in Central Europe. It is as though Goethe were saying in *Götz von Berlichingen* that intellectualism has seized hold of Central Europe too. But here it appears as something that is out of place. It would not have occurred to Goethe to negate Shakespeare. We know how positive was Goethe's attitude to Shakespeare. It would not have occurred to him to find fault with Shakespeare, because his work led to a satisfying culmination which could be allowed to stand. On the contrary, he found this extraordinarily satisfying.

But the way in which intellectualism developed in his own environment made Goethe depict its existence as something unjustified, whereas he spiritually embraced the political element of what was expressed in the French Revolution. In *Götz von Berlichingen* Goethe is the spiritual revolutionary who denies the spirit in the same way as the French Revolution denies the political element. Goethe turns back in a certain way to something that has once been, though he certainly cannot wish that it should return in its old form. He wants it to develop in a different direction. It is most interesting to observe this mood in Goethe, this mood of revolt against what has come to replace the world of Götz.

So it is extremely interesting to find that Shakespeare has been so deeply grasped by Lessing and by Goethe and that they really followed on from Shakespeare in seeking what they wanted to find through their mood of spiritual revolt. Yet where intellectualism has become particularly deeply entrenched, for instance in Voltaire, it mounts a most virulent attack on Shakespeare. We know that Voltaire called Shakespeare a wild drunkard. All these things have to be taken into account.

Now add something else to the great question which is so important for an understanding of the spiritual revolution which took place in the transition from the fourth to the fifth post-Atlantean period. Add to all this the extraordinary part which Schiller played in this spiritual revolution which in Goethe is expressed in a Goethean way in *Götz von Berlichingen*. In the circle closest of all to Schiller he first met what he had to revolt against. It came out of the most one-sided, unhealthy intellectualism. There was of course as yet no Waldorf school to do battle against one-sided intellectualism. So Schiller could not be sent to the Waldorf school in Wurttemberg but had to go to the Karlsschule instead. All the protest which Schiller built up during his youth grew out of his protest against the education he received at the Karlsschule. This kind of education—Schiller wrote his drama *Die Räuber* against it—is now universally accepted, and no positive, really productive opposition to it has ever been mounted until the recent foundation of the Waldorf school.

So what is the position of Schiller—who later stood beside Goethe—in all this? He writes *Die Räuber*. It is perfectly obvious to those who can judge such things that in Spiegelberg and the other characters he has portrayed his fellow pupils. Franz Moor himself could not so easily be derived from his schoolmates, but in Franz Moor he has shown in an ahrimanic form everything that his genius can grasp of what lives in his time. If you know how to look at these things, you can see how Schiller does not depict spiritual beings externally, in the way they appear in *Hamlet* or *Macbeth*, but that he allows the ahrimanic principle to work in Franz Moor. And opposite this is the luciferic principle in Karl Moor. In Franz Moor we see a representative of all that Schiller is rebelling against. It is the same world against which Goethe is rebelling in *Götz von Berlichingen*, only Schiller sets about it in a different way. We see this too in the later drama *Kabale und Liebe*.

So you see that here in Central Europe these spirits, Goethe and Schiller, do not depict something in the way Shakespeare does. They do not allow events to lead to something with which one can come to terms. They depict something which is there but which in their opinion ought to have developed quite differently. What they really want does not exist, and what is there on the physical plane is something which they oppose in a spiritual revolution. So we have a strange interplay between what exists on the physical plane and what lives in these spirits.

Lecture 2   63

```
red                                              blue
```

In a rather bold way I could draw it. In Shakespeare the events he depicts carry on in keeping with the way things are on earth (blue). What he takes in from earlier times, in which the spirit still worked, goes over (red) into a present time which then becomes a factual world evolution.

```
red                                              blue
```

Then we see in Goethe and Schiller that they had inklings of an earlier time (red) when the spiritual world was still powerful, in the fourth post-Atlantean period, and that they bring this only as far as their spiritual intentions, whereas they see what is taking place on earth (blue) as being in conflict with it. One thing plays into the other in the human struggle for the spirit. This is why here in Central Europe the question became a purely human one. In the time of Goethe and Schiller a tremendous revolution occurred in the concept of man as a being who stands within a social context. I shall be able to expand on this in the coming lectures.

Let us now look towards the eastern part of Europe. But we cannot look in that direction in the same way. Those who only describe external facts and have no understanding for what lives in the souls of Goethe and Schiller—and also of course many others—may describe these facts very well, but they will fail to include what plays in from a spiritual world—which is certainly also there, although it may be present only in the heads of human beings. In France the battle takes place on the physical earth, in a political revolution. In Germany the battle does not come down as far as the physical plane. It comes down as far as human souls and trembles and vibrates there. But we cannot continue this consideration in the same way with regard to the East, for things are different there. If we want to pursue the matter with regard to the East we need to call on the assistance of anthroposophy. For what takes place in the souls of Goethe and Schiller, which are after all, here on the earth—what, in them, blows through earthly souls is, in the East, still in the spiritual world and finds no expression whatsoever down on the earth.

If you want to describe what took place between Goethe's and Schiller's spirits in the physical world—if you want to describe this with regard to the East, then you will have to employ a different view, such as that used in the days of Attila when battles were fought by spirits in the air above the heads of human beings.

What you find being carried out in Europe by Goethe and Schiller—Schiller by writing *Die Räuber* and Goethe by writing *Götz von Berlichingen*—you will find in the East to be taking place as a spiritual fact in the spiritual world above the physical plane. If you want to seek deeds which parallel the writing of *Die Räuber* and the writing of *Götz*, you will have to seek them among the spiritual beings of the supersensible world. There is no point in searching for them on the physical plane. In a diagram depicting what happens in the East you would have to draw the element in question like a cloud floating above the physical plane, while down below, untouched by it, would be what shows externally on the physical plane.

red /////////////////////

blue /////////////////////

Now we know that, because we have Hamlet, we can tell how a western human being who had been a pupil of Faust would have behaved, and could have behaved. But there can be no such thing as a Russian Hamlet. Or can there? We could see a Russian Hamlet with our spiritual eyes if we were to imagine the following. Faust lectures at Wittenberg—I mean not the historical Faust but Goethe's Faust who is actually more true than historical fact. Faust lectures at Wittenberg—and Hamlet listens, writing everything down, just as he does even what the ghost says to him about the villains who live in Denmark. He writes everything down in the book and volume of his brain—Shakespeare created a true pupil of Faust out of what he found in the work of Saxo Grammaticus, which depicts things quite differently. Now imagine that an angel being also listened to Faust as he lectured—Hamlet sat on the university bench, Faust stood on the platform, and at the back of the lecture hall an angel listened. And this angel then flew to the East and there brought about what could have taken place as a parallel to the deeds of Hamlet in the West.

I do not believe that it is possible to reach a truly penetrating comprehension of these things by solely taking account of external facts. One cannot ignore the very profound impression made, by these external facts, particularly on the greatest personalities of the time, when what is taking place is something as incisive as the spiritual revolution which took place between the fourth and fifth post-Atlantean periods.

Lecture 3

STRATFORD-ON-AVON, 23 APRIL 1922*

From the announcement of the theme of today's lecture 'Shakespeare and the New Ideals', it might be expected that I would speak, above all, about new ideals. But I am convinced that it is not so necessary to speak of new ideals today as it is to speak of a wider question, namely the following: How are men and women of our time to regain the power to follow ideals? After all, no great power is required to speak about ideals; indeed, it is often the case that those who speak most about these great questions, expanding beautiful ideals in abstract words out of their intellect, are those who lack the very power to put ideals into practice. Sometimes, speaking of ideals amounts to no more than holding onto illusions in the mind in order to pass over life's realities.

At this festival, however, we have every cause to speak of what is spiritual as a reality. For this festival commemorates Shakespeare, and Shakespeare lives in what is spiritual in all that he created; he lives in it as in a real world. Receiving Shakespeare into our minds and souls might therefore be the very stimulus to give us men and women of today the power, the inner impulse to follow ideals, to follow real, spiritual ideals. We shall see our true ideals aright if we bear in mind

---

* Many gaps exist in the notes to this lecture, but because of the lack of a shorthand version it was impossible to check it for accuracy.

how transitory many modern ideals have been and are, and how magnificently firm are many old ideals that still hold their own in the world by their effectiveness. Do we not see wide circles of believers in this or that religion who base their innermost spiritual life and their inner mobility of spirit on something of the past, and gain from it the power of spiritual upliftment? And so we ask how is it that many modern ideals, beautiful as they are, and held for a while with great enthusiasm by large numbers of people, before long vanish as into a cloud, whereas religious or artistic ideals of old carry their full force into humanity not just through centuries but even through millennia?

If we ask this question, we are brought back repeatedly to the fact that, whereas our modern ideals are generally no more than shadow pictures of the intellect, the old ideals were garnered from real spiritual life, from a definite spirituality inherent in the humanity of the time. The intellect can never give human beings real power from the depths of their being. And, because this is so, many modern ideals vanish and fade away long before what speaks to us, through the old religious faiths, or through the old styles of art, from hoary antiquity.

Returning to Shakespeare with these thoughts in mind, we know that a power lives in his dramatic work that not only always gives us fresh enthusiasm but also kindles within us—in our imaginations, in our spiritual natures—our own creative powers. Shakespeare has a wonderfully timeless power and, in this power, he is modern, as modern as can be.

Here, from the point of view of the connection between human ideals and Shakespeare, I might perhaps call to mind what I mentioned last Wednesday, namely Shakespeare's deeply significant influence on Goethe. Countless books and treatises have been written on Shakespeare out of academic cleverness—exceptional cleverness. Taking all of the learned works on *Hamlet* alone, I think that one could fill library shelves that would cover this wall. But, when we seek to find what it was in Shakespeare that worked on such a man as Goethe, we finally come to the conclusion that absolutely nothing relating to that is contained in all that has been written in these books. They could have remained unwritten. All of the effort that has been brought to bear on Shakespeare stems from the world of the human intellect, which is certainly good for understanding facts of natural science and for giving such an explanation of external nature as we need to found for our modern technical achievements, but which can never penetrate what stands livingly and movingly before us in Shakespeare's plays.

Indeed, I could go further. Goethe, too, from this standpoint of intellectual understanding, wrote many things on Shakespeare's plays by way of explanation—on *Hamlet*, for example—and all of this, too, that Goethe wrote is, in the main, one-sided and barren. However, what matters is not what Goethe said about Shakespeare but what he meant when he spoke from his inmost experience, for example, when he said, 'These are no mere poems! It is as though the great leaves of fate were opened and the storm-wind of life were blowing through them, turning them quickly to and fro.' These words are no explanation, but voice the devotion of his spirit. Spoken from his own humanity, they are very different from what he himself wrote by way of explanation about *Hamlet*.

Now, we might ask, why is it that Shakespeare is so difficult to approach intellectually? I shall try to give an answer in a picture. Someone has a vivid dream in which the characters enact a whole incident before the dreamer. Looking back on it later with the intellect, she or he might say that this or that figure in the dream acted wrongly; here is an action without motive or continuity, here are contradictions. But the dream cares little for such criticism. Just as little will the poet care how we criticize with our intellect and whether we find actions contradictory or inconsistent. I once knew a pedantic critic who found it strange that Hamlet, having only just seen the ghost of his father before him, should speak the monologue, 'To be or not to be', saying in it that 'no traveller returns' from the land of death. This, the man of learning thought, was really absurd! I do not mean to say that Shakespeare's dramatic scenes are dream scenes. Shakespeare experiences his scenes in full, living consciousness. They are as conscious as can be. But he uses the intellect only in so far as it serves him to develop his characters, to unfold them, to give form to action. He does not make his intellect master of what is to happen in his scenes.

I speak here from the anthroposophical view of the world. This view, I believe, does contain the great ideals of humanity. Perhaps, therefore, I may mention at this point a significant experience that explains fully—by means of 'artistic seership'—something that was first known through feeling. I have already had occasion to speak about the way in which 'exact clairvoyance' is being cultivated at the Goetheanum, the school of spiritual science in Dornach, Switzerland. I have described the paths to this exact clairvoyance in the books translated into English as *How to Know Higher Worlds*, *Theosophy*, and *An Outline of Occult Science*. By means of certain exercises, carried out no less precisely than in the learning of mathematics, we can strengthen our soul faculties. Gradually, we can so develop our powers of thought, feeling and will that we are able to live with our souls consciously—not in the unconsciousness of sleep or in dreams—outside the body. We become able to leave behind the physical body with its intellectualistic thought—for this remains with the physical body—in full consciousness. Then we have 'imaginations', by which I do not mean such fanciful imaginings as are justified in artistic work, but I mean *true imaginations*, true pictures of the spiritual world surrounding us. Through what I have called 'Imagination', 'Inspiration', and 'Intuition', we learn to perceive in the spiritual world. Just as we consciously perceive this physical world and, through our senses, learn to build an understanding of it as a totality from the single sensory impressions of sound and colour, so from the spiritual perceptions of exact clairvoyance we learn to build up an understanding of the spiritual world as a totality. Exact clairvoyance has nothing to do with hallucinations and illusions that enter a human being pathologically, always clouding and decreasing consciousness. In exact clairvoyance, we come to know the spiritual world in full consciousness, as clearly and as exactly as when we do mathematical work. Transferring ourselves into high spiritual regions, we experience pictures comparable, not with what are ordinarily known as visions, but rather with memory pictures. But these are pictures of an absolutely real spiritual world.

All of the original ideals of humanity in science, art, and religion were derived from the spiritual world. That is why the old ideals have a greater, more impelling power than modern intellectual ideals. The old ideals were seen in the spiritual world through clairvoyance, a clairvoyance that was at that time more instinctive and dreamlike. They were derived and taken from a spiritual source. By all means let us recognize quite clearly that certain contents of religious faith are no longer suited to our time. They have been handed down from ancient times. We need once more wide-open doors to look into the spiritual world and to take thence, not such abstract ideals as are spoken of on every side, but the power to follow the ideal and the spiritual in science, in art, and in religion.

If we approach Shakespeare with such powers of seeing into the spiritual world, we shall experience something quite specific, and it is of this that I wish to speak. Shakespeare can be understood with true and artistic feeling; exact clairvoyance is, of course, not necessary to have a full experience of his power. But exact clairvoyance can show us something most significant, which will explain why it is that Shakespeare can never let us feel he has left us, why it is that he is forever giving us fresh force and impulse. It is this: whoever has attained exact clairvoyance by developing the powers of thought, feeling and will can carry over into the spiritual world what we have experienced here of Shakespeare. This is possible. What we have experienced here in the physical body—let us say that we have been entering deeply into the character of Hamlet or Macbeth—we can take this experience over into the spiritual world. We can see what lived in

Shakespeare's deep inner life only when we compare it with the impressions that we are able to take over into the spiritual world from poets of more modern times. I do not wish to mention any particular poet by name—I know that everyone has his or her favourite poets—but any one of the naturalistic poets, particularly of recent years, could be mentioned. If we compare what we take over from Shakespeare with what we have in the spiritual world from these poets, we discover the remarkable fact that Shakespeare's characters live! When we take them over into the spiritual world, they act. They act differently, but they bring their life here into the spiritual world. Whereas, if we take over the characters created by a modern naturalistic poet into the spiritual world, they really behave more like dolls than human beings! They have no life in them at all, no movement! Shakespeare's men and women keep their life and character. But the characters of many other poets, derived from naturalism, are just like wooden dolls in the spiritual world! They go through a kind of freezing process! Indeed, we ourselves are chilled by contact with such modern poetry in the spiritual world.

I am not saying this out of any kind of emotion, but as a matter of experience. With this experience in mind, we may ask again: What was it that Goethe felt? 'It is as though the great book of fate is opened in Shakespeare, and life's stormy wind is turning its pages quickly to and fro.' Goethe knew and felt how Shakespeare created from the full depths of the spiritual world. This has given Shakespeare his real immortality: this makes him ever new. We can go through a play of Shakespeare's and experience it ten, twenty, a hundred times!

Ladies and gentlemen, you have had before you within the last few days the scene from *Much Ado about Nothing* where the Friar kneels down beside the fallen heroine and utters his conviction of her innocence. It is something unspeakably deep and true, and there is hardly anything in modern literature to be compared with it. Indeed, it is most often the intimate touches in Shakespeare that work with such power and reveal his inner life and vitality.

Or again, in *As You Like It* where the Duke stands before the trees and all of the life of nature in the Forest of Arden and says that they are better counsellors than those at court, for they tell him something of what he is as a human being. What a wonderful perception of nature speaks from the whole of this well-known passage! '... tongues in trees, books in the running brooks...' Here is an understanding of nature, here is a reading of nature! It is true that the more modern poets can also indicate such things, but we often feel that in them it is something second-hand. In Shakespeare, we feel that he is himself everything. Even when they both say the same, it is altogether different whether Shakespeare says it or some other poet.

Thus the great question comes before us: How is it that, in Shakespeare, there is this living quality that is so intimately related to the supersensible? Whence comes the life in Shakespeare's dramas? This question leads us to see how Shakespeare, working as he did in the sixteenth and seventeenth centuries, was able to create something that still had living connections with the life of the most ancient drama. And this most ancient drama, as it speaks to us from Aeschylus, from Sophocles, is in turn a product of the mysteries, those ancient cultic, artistic actions that derive from the most ancient, instinctive, inner spiritual knowledge. We can understand what inspires us so in true art, if we seek the origin of art in the mysteries.

If I now make some brief remarks on the ancient mysteries as the source of the artistic sense and artistic creative power, the objection can of course very easily be made that what is said on this subject from the standpoint of exact clairvoyance is unsupported by sufficient proof. Exact clairvoyance, however, brings us into touch not only with what surrounds us at the present day but also, most emphatically, with the world of history, with the historical evolution of humanity, and of the universe. Those who follow the method that I have described in my books can themselves investigate what exact clairvoyance has to say upon the subject of the mysteries.

When speaking of the mysteries, we are looking back into very ancient times in human evolution, times when religion, art, and science did not yet stand separately, side by side, as they do today. Generally, people are insufficiently aware of the changes—the metamorphoses—that art, religion and science have undergone before reaching the separation and differentiation that they experience today. I will mention only one thing to indicate how, to some extent, modern anthroposophical knowledge brings us into contact again with older forms of true artistic life.

Across the centuries, the works of earlier painters—those, say, before the end of the thirteenth and during the fourteenth centuries—come down to us. We need only think of Cimabue. Thereafter, something that has rightly held sway in modern painting enters into painting. This is what we call perspective. In the paintings in the dome of the Goetheanum in Switzerland, you can see how we are returning once again to the perspective which lies in the colours themselves—where we have a different feeling in the blue, the red and the yellow. It is as though we were leaving the ordinary physical world: the third dimension of space ceases to have significance, and we work in two dimensions only.

Thus, a painter can return to a connection with the ancient instinctive spiritual experience of humanity. It is this possibility that modern anthroposophy seeks to give through all that I have said concerning exact clairvoyance.

Looking back at the life of ancient, instinctive clairvoyance, we find it connected equally with the artistic, the religious, and the scientific; that is, with the whole of the ancient form of knowledge. There was always an understanding for the union of religion, art and science—which in those days meant a revelation of divine cosmic forces—in the mystery cults. In so far as they were a manifestation of divine forces, the mystery cults entered deeply into humanity's religious feelings; in so far as they were already what we call today artistic—what we cultivate in art—they were the works of art for the people of that time. And, in so far as those ancient peoples were aware that true knowledge is gained not by seeking it one-sidedly through the head but through the experience of the whole being, the ancient mysteries in their development were also mediators for human knowledge as it then was. Today, on the other hand, according to the modern view, knowledge can be acquired simply by taking ordinary consciousness—remaining as we are—and observing nature, forming concepts from the facts of nature.

Our modern way of approaching the world in order to gain knowledge of it is not the same as it was in ancient times. In the old way, to look into the spiritual world, one had to lift oneself to a higher level of one's humanity. Of course, this ancient way of knowing was not the same as our present exact clairvoyance. Nevertheless, the human being did see into the spiritual world. The mystery rites were enacted, not to display something for the outer eye, but to awaken inner experience in the whole human being. Mighty destinies formed the subject of these mystery rites. Through them, human beings were brought to forget their ordinary selves. They were lifted out of ordinary life. Although in a dream and not as clearly as is required today, they entered the state of living outside their bodies. That was the purpose of the mysteries. By the witness of deeply moving scenes and actions, the mysteries sought to bring the neophyte to the point of living and experiencing outside the physical body.

There are certain fundamental experiences characteristic of life outside the body. One great experience is the following. In the physical body, our ordinary life of feeling is interwoven with the organic processes in our own body. But when we are outside the body, our feeling encompasses everything that surrounds us. We experience in feeling all of the life around us. Imagine that a person is outside the physical body with his or her soul and spiritual life and experiences spiritually—not with the intellect's ice-cold forces but with the forces of the soul, with feeling and emotion. Imagine what it feels like to experience outside the body in this way. It is a great sympathy with all things—with thunder and lightning, with the rippling of the stream, the welling forth of the river spring, the sighing of the wind—and a feeling of togetherness also with other human beings, as well as with the spiritual entities of the world. Outside the body, one learns to know this great empathy.

Now, united with this great feeling of empathy, another fundamental feeling also comes over the human being in the face of what is at first unknown. I refer to a certain sense of fear. These two feelings—the feeling of empathy with all the world, and the feeling of fear—played a great part in the ancient mysteries. When the pupils had strengthened themselves in their inner lives so that they were able, without turning away and without losing their inner control, to bear both the living empathy with the world and the fear, then they were ripe enough and sufficiently evolved really to see into the spiritual worlds. They were then ready to live and experience the spiritual world. And they were ready, too, to communicate to their fellow human beings knowledge drawn from spiritual worlds. With their feeling, they could work down from the spiritual worlds into this world, and a new poetic power was revealed in their speech. Their hands became skilled to work in colours; they were able to command the inner rhythm of their organism so that they could become musicians for the benefit of other human beings. In this way, they became artists. They could hand down from the mysteries what the primeval religions gave to humanity. Anyone who looks into the Catholic Mass with inner spiritual knowledge knows that it is the last shadowlike reflection of what was living in the mysteries.

At first, what was living in the mysteries had its artistic and its religious side. Afterward, these two separated. In

Aeschylus and in Sophocles we already see the artistic element, as it were, lifted out of the mysteries. There is the divine hero, Prometheus. In Prometheus, the human being comes to know something of the deeply moving, terrifying experiences, the inner fear of the mysteries. What was living in the mysteries, in which the neophytes were initiated into a higher stage of life, becomes in Prometheus a picture, though permeated with living dramatic power. Thus drama became an image of the deepest human experiences. Aristotle, who was already, in a sense, an intellectual, still lived in some of the old traditions. He knew and experienced how drama was a kind of echo of the ancient mysteries. For this reason, Aristotle said, putting into words what was an echo of the ancient mysteries living on in Aeschylus and Sophocles, what has been dismissed by learned men again and again in their books: 'Drama is the representation of a scene calling forth sympathy and fear, in order that human beings may be purified of physical passions, that they may undergo catharsis.' We cannot understand what this catharsis, or purification, means unless we look back into the ancient mysteries and see how people were purified of what is physical and lived through mighty experiences in the supersensible, outside their physical bodies. Aristotle describes what had already become a picture in Greek drama. Afterwards, this passed over to later dramatists, and we see in Corneille and Racine something that is a fulfilment of Aristotle's words. We see characters clothed, as it were, in fear and compassion—compassion that is none other than the ancient sympathy and experience with all the world that the human being experienced outside the body. The fear is always there when the human being faces the unknown. The supersensible is always, in a sense, the unknown.

Shakespeare entered into the evolution of drama in his time. He entered into a world that was seeking a new dramatic element. Something transcending ordinary human life lives in drama. Shakespeare entered deeply into this. He was inspired by that ancient dramatic power which, to a certain extent, was still felt by his contemporaries. And he worked in such a way that we feel in Shakespeare that more than a single human personality is at work: the spirit of his century is at work and, with it, the spirit of the whole of human evolution. Shakespeare still lived in that ancient feeling, and so he called something to life in himself that enabled him to form his dramatic characters and human figures not in any intellectual way but by living right within them himself. The characters of Shakespeare's plays come not from human intellect but from a power kindled and fired in the human being. It is this power that we must seek again if we would develop the true ideal of humanity.

Let us come back to the unification of art, science and religion. This is our aim at the Goetheanum in Dornach. By the development of exact clairvoyance, we come to understand what was at work in the ancient mysteries. The element that the mystery dramatists placed, as yet externally, before their audiences was still at work in Shakespeare who recreated it in a wonderfully inward way.

It is no mere outer feature of Shakespeare's plays that we find in them about a hundred and fifty names of different plants and about a hundred names of birds, everywhere intimately, lovingly interwoven with human life. All of this is part of the single whole in Shakespeare.

Shakespeare took the continuous current that flows through human evolution from the ancient mysteries—their cults and rites—wholly into his inner life. He took this impulse of the ancient mysteries and his plays come forth like dreams that are awake and real. The intellect with its explanations, its consistencies and inconsistencies, cannot approach them. As little as we can apply intellectual standards to a Prometheus or an Oedipus, just so little can we apply them to Shakespeare's plays.

Thus, in a wonderful way, we can see in Shakespeare's own person a development that we can call a mystery development. Shakespeare comes to London where he draws on historical traditions for his material. In his plays, he is still dependent on others. We see then how, from about 1598 onwards, a certain inner life awakens. Shakespeare's own artistic imagination comes to life. He is able to stamp his characters with the very interior of his being. Sometime later, when he has created *Hamlet*, a kind of bitterness towards the external physical world comes over him. We feel as though he were living in other worlds and judging the physical world differently—as though he were looking down from the point of view of other worlds. We then see him emerge from this inner deepening of experience with all of its inner tragedy. First, Shakespeare learns the external dramatic medium. Next, he goes through deepest inwardness—what I would call the meeting with the World Spirit, of which Goethe spoke so beautifully. Then he re-enters life with a certain humour, and his work carries with it the loftiest spirituality joined with the highest dramatic power. Here, I am thinking, for example, of *The Tempest,* one of the most wonderful creations of all humankind, one of the richest products of the evolution of dramatic art. In it, Shakespeare, in a living, human way, is able to lay his ripe philosophy of life into every character and figure.

So, having seen the art of drama derive from the ancient mysteries whose purpose was the living evolution of humanity, we can understand how it is that such an educational power goes out from Shakespeare's plays. We can see how Shakespeare's work, which arose out of a kind of self-education given by nature herself, which he then lifted to the highest spirituality, can work in our schools and penetrate the living education of our youth. Once we have thus experienced their full cosmic spirituality, Shakespeare's dramas must be livingly present with us when we consider the great educational questions of the day. But we must be active with all of the means at our disposal, for only by the deepest spirituality shall we find in Shakespeare the answer to these questions.

Such are the ideals that humanity needs so sorely. We have a wonderful natural science in our time, but it places a world that is dense and material before us. It can teach us nothing else than the final end of it all in a kind of universal death. And when we consider natural evolution, as it is given to us in the thoughts of the last centuries, it seems like something strange and foreign when we look up to our spiritual ideals. So we ask whether the religious ideal has a real force, adequate to the needs of the civilized world today. But it has not. We must regain this real force by rising to the spiritual world. Only then, by spiritual knowledge and not by mere belief, shall we find the strength in our ideals to overcome all material aspects in the cosmos. We must be able to lift ourselves up to the power that creates from truly religious ideals, the power to overcome the world of matter in the universe. We can do this only if we yield ourselves to the spiritual conception of the world and, for this, Shakespeare can be a great leader. Moreover, it is an intense social need that there be a spiritual conception of the world working in our time. Do not think I am speaking out of egotism when I refer once again to Dornach in Switzerland, where we are cultivating what can lead humanity once more into the reality of the spiritual, into the true spiritual nature of the world. Only because of this were we able to overcome many of those contending interests working in people today and so sadly splitting them into parties and differing sections in every sphere of life. I could mention that, from 1913 until now, almost without a break, through the whole period of the war, while nearby the thunder of the cannon was heard, members of no less than 17 nations have been working together in Dornach. That 17 nations could work together peacefully during the greatest of all wars, this, too, seems to me a great ideal in education. What is possible on a small scale should be possible on a large scale, and human progress—human civilization—needs it. And, precisely because we favour an international advance in human civilization, I point to Shakespeare as a figure who worked in all humanity. He gave all humanity a great inspiration for new human ideals, ideals that have a meaning for international, universal humanity.

Therefore, let me close on this festival day with these

words of Goethe, words that Goethe was impelled to speak when he felt the fullness of the spirituality in Shakespeare. There then arose from his heart a saying that, I think, must set its stamp on all our understanding of the great poet, who will remain an eternal source of inspiration to all. Conscious of this, Goethe uttered these words on Shakespeare with which we may close our thoughts today: 'It is the nature of spirit to inspire spirit eternally.' Hence, we may rightly say, 'Shakespeare for ever and without end!'

Rudolf Steiner's Report on the Stratford Shakespeare Festival in 1922

In this connection I was permitted to state my anthroposophical point of view regarding Shakespeare, education, and the requirements of the spiritual life today. One of the ways in which the educational power of Shakespeare's art is involved in the history of human evolution is through the influence that Shakespeare's art exerted upon Goethe. The question must be asked: Upon what does this tremendous influence rest?

When I ask myself this question, I am confronted by a fact in supersensible experience. Anyone who is in a position to devote himself livingly to Shakespeare's dramas and then carry this experience into that world which spreads out before 'exact clairvoyance' can find that the figures of Shakespeare's dramas continue to appear before the soul in the supersensible realm as living, whereas the figures out of the new naturalistic dramas are either transformed completely through this process into puppets or, in a sense, become immobile. In Imagination, Shakespeare's figures continue to live. They do not continue to carry out the same actions as in the dramas; rather, they act in different situations and with a changed course of factual events. I believe this indicates that Shakespeare's figures are deeply rooted in the spiritual world, and that Goethe, in his devotion to Shakespearean drama, unconsciously experienced this fact of their being deeply rooted. When he turned to Shakespeare,

Goethe felt as if he himself were seized upon by events of the spirit world. I had this experience in the back of my mind when I had the opportunity to speak in Stratford about Shakespeare, Goethe, and the nature of education in three lectures. My conviction of this was especially vivid when I spoke on 23 April, the real Shakespeare Day, about 'Shakespeare and the New Ideals'.

The programmes arranged by the committee for 'New Ideals in Education' were accompanied by presentations of Shakespeare dramas in the Shakespeare Memorial Theatre. We had the opportunity to see *Othello, Julius Caesar, The Taming of the Shrew, Twelfth Night, All's Well that Ends Well* and *Much Ado about Nothing*.

The presentation of the comedies was satisfying, but I have a different conception of the right presentation of the tragedies.

Editor's Acknowledgements

With much gratitude do I acknowledge my indebtedness to those who have been part of the process that has led to this publication: Nathaniel Bowron, one of my teachers in Kings Langley, who first awakened in me that a Shakespeare text is sacrosanct and should not be shortened for the convenience of performance considerations; Theodore Nicholl, who lovingly guided my literature studies for A levels and patiently bore and wisely schooled my juvenile interpretations; Francis Edmunds, whose passion for Shakespeare confirmed my own; Dawn Langman, whose illuminating and penetrating insights have nourished so many conversations and my work; Sylvia Eckersley, whose companionable presence and dedicated perseverance with her Shakespeare research accompanied me since I was a child; Richard Ramsbotham, whose love of the truth in the authorship question awoke my own better understanding; Sarah Kane, who guided me to understand the beauty of the truth in the metre; Sarah Kane and Richard Ramsbotham, for many years of exemplary and exuberant colleagueship; and all my students, who over many continents and many years have shared with me their questions, comments and trust, and supported my own growth in all this.

My inestimable gratitude to Rudolf Steiner is, I trust, apparent in the body of this publication.

Andrew Wolpert